NEEDLECRAFT

Betty Showler
Gwendoline Strafford
Angela Thompson
Beaujolois I. Cavendish

Consultant: Pat Cherry
NFWI Home Economics Adviser

BOOK CLUB ASSOCIATES
LONDON

Designed and created by
Berkeley Publishers Ltd.
9 Warwick Court
London WC1 R 5DJ

Editor Gaynor Cauter
Design Gudrun Finnsdottir
 and Barbara Mercer
Photography Chris Ridley
Crown Copyright: Victoria and
 Albert Museum
Ann Ronan Picture Library
Illustrations David Parr

Air Electronic kindly lent by
Elna Sewing Machines (G.B.)
Ltd.

First published 1979
Macdonald Educational Ltd.
Holywell House
Worship Street
London EC2A 2EN

This edition published 1979 by
Book Club Associates
By arrangement with
Macdonald Educational Ltd.

Editorial manager
Chester Fisher
Publishing co-ordinator
Robin Cross
Production manager
Eva Wrennall

Made and printed by
Purnell & Sons Ltd.
Paulton

Contents

Introduction

The last few years have witnessed a new surge of interest in home crafts of all kinds, creating a demand for information about both traditional and modern techniques in the fields of needlecraft and creative handiwork. It has taken centuries for such skills to develop throughout the world, from the traditional patchwork of North America to the fine rug stitching techniques of the Far East.

Now machinery is taking over so much of what was once created so beautifully by hand, we are in danger of losing the knowledge of those skills which were once commonly practised in the ordinary home. But this does not mean that today's technology cannot be used to complement those ancient skills. Although tastes and fashions change over the centuries, it is possible to harmonize time-honoured patterns with modern tastes in colour and design.

The National Federation of Women's Institutes has always sought to revive and maintain those crafts and creative skills which are continually threatened by modern technology. As Britain's biggest women's organization, the NFWI is in a unique position to do this and its craftswomen members have gained a considerable reputation.

This book presents four traditional skills in a thoroughly modern manner. Patchwork was traditionally a purely practical and economical way of making use of scraps of material from worn-out clothing, too valuable to throw away. Gradually ornamental motifs and patterns were incorporated until patchwork became an art form in itself and specific and recognizable patterns and designs emerged, the names of which are now part of any patchwork maker's vocabulary.

Canvas work is a centuries-old form of embroidery, worked with wool in a variety of stitches which all adapt happily to modern colours and designs, using readily available materials. Family emblems, heraldic motifs, geometric patterns and impressionist designs can all be beautifully applied to canvas with great effect.

Machine embroidery is possibly the ultimate example of harmony between ancient and modern. It is a skill in its own right, combining the great traditions of embroidery with the precision engineering of the modern sewing machine. Even a simple swing-needle machine can be transformed into a tool capable of creating a vast range of different patterns and designs. A little practice and concentration will produce the most satisfying results.

Stitched rugs easily adapt to every extreme of colour and design, from the spectacular colours of the hardy Scandinavian Rya, with its shaggy pile, to the intricate details of oriental designs and the subtle sophistication of traditional patterns. In common with canvas work, stitched rug making is a skill which allows for the tiniest details to be represented neatly and effectively.

The authors of each section of this book are all experts in their field with years of practical experience behind them. Techniques are carefully explained and illustrated with detailed line drawings and colour pictures of the finished articles.

Each one of these skills has its own special fascination —a fascination which has ensured its survival over the centuries. This book not only explains basic techniques to the beginner but it can also be used with pleasure by the skilled craftsman.

Pat Cherry

NFWI Home Economics Adviser

Things of beauty
-from small scraps

Patchwork may be said to have grown from necessity. In the old days no thrifty housewife threw scraps of material away. They were saved up and turned into beautifully matched and patterned quilts. Today patchwork is widely recognized as one of the most delightful of all the old craft skills and is enjoying a well-deserved revival. The really good patchwork quilt is a work of art in its own right and gives a touch of hand–made luxury to any bedroom.

Patchwork beauty from odd scraps

The patchwork that most of us recognize is pieced patchwork, which uses odd pieces of material, cut into geometric or irregular shapes and joined together to make up a mosaic surface. It is an ancient thrift craft, carried out in the home. The current revival of interest in creative handcraft is adding yet another chapter to its long history. Evidence indicates that it was practised in ancient Egypt.

Cairo Museum has a funeral pall, 3,000 years old which is believed to be the oldest patchwork in existence, but as much of the decoration is applied it also establishes the close association of patchwork with appliqué. We know that the crusaders' gaily patterned banners were made of applied materials brought home from Italy and the Low Countries.

In England patchwork has been practised for centuries, influenced by social conditions, and used to portray historic events in each period.

The importation of gaily coloured cotton chintz from India towards the end of the seventeenth century provided excellent, long lasting fabrics which were soon incorporated into patchwork. Levens Hall, near Kendal, Lancashire, houses a fine bedcover made at that time. The work is composed of patches of five different shapes joined in a repetitive pattern. The bedcover is quilted with a red thread.

When importation of these popular fabrics was limited, every fragment left over from dressmaking was preserved to make up furnishings in patchwork. Patterned material was often augmented with white or unbleached calico. Imagination and discipline were necessary and an appreciation of the value of plain, unpatterned areas in design was a very characteristic feature of the eighteenth and early nineteenth century.

Most of the work handed down

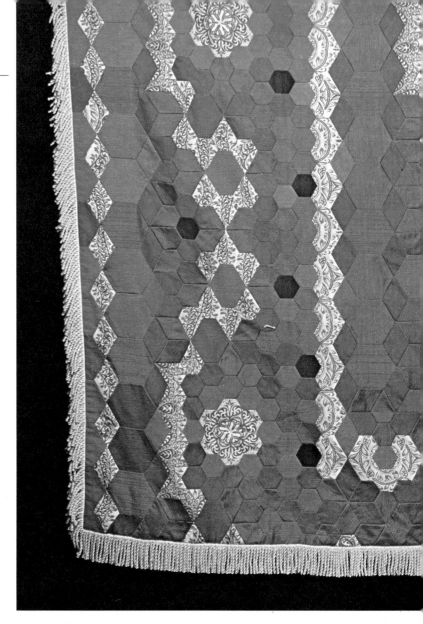

to us dates from after the mid-eighteenth century, which was an outstanding period for English patchwork. The majority of the work was made into bedcovers. It often involved quilting, for extra warmth, with smaller items made for personal wear or in the form of cushions for the home.

Patchwork for decorative use only became fashionable in the late Victorian and Edwardian periods and took less durable forms, like crazy work and Suffolk puffs. Indeed there were few houses of that period that did not boast a cushion or even a quilt in crazy work. In needlewomen's homes these examples would be highly decorated with embroidery as well as with top

stitchery connecting the patches.

In the period after the first world war, patchwork declined from its fashion status and reverted to its original function as a thrift craft. But today our lives are filled with the colour and pattern of patchwork as no other time has offered such a variety of readily available and suitable materials.

The story of patchwork in America is much written about. It is said that the history of the United States of America is written in its patchwork quilts, for the craft has been part of home and social life ever since the early settlers left Europe to establish themselves on the East Coast. It is still widely practised especially in the country

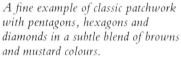

A fine example of classic patchwork with pentagons, hexagons and diamonds in a subtle blend of browns and mustard colours.

majority are worked in appliqué, a few are pieced patchwork, or a mixture of appliqué and patchwork.

Patchwork was often made up by a group of women getting together in a quilting party or sewing bee, and no doubt gossip added a fresh dimension to the work. One is apt to regard these quilting parties as peculiar to America, but in England too, in the past as the present, work has been shared by families or groups. Jane Austen helped her mother and sisters in the making of a quilt. Work is still being done by communal effort. A group of Surrey Women's Institute members made a quilt for the Queen in celebration of her Silver Jubilee.

Patchwork has much to offer today, the chance to perfect a technical skill, to explore colour and shape in relation to the division of the surface with enormous variety of combination, to fulfil a creative outlet, which may not be satisfied in everyday life, as well as producing a useful article for the home or as an acceptable gift.

Equipment

Patchwork is a plain sewing craft, so a well equipped work basket will provide most of the materials needed. A recommended list of equipment required is:

Needles No. 9 or 10 Betweens for fine sewing; No. 6 or 7 Betweens for tacking purposes

Fine pins Dressmakers, lace or Lills (Lillikins)

Thread Fine sewing cotton, white or black, 80 or 100, or Gütermann M303 100 per cent polyester cotton White tacking cotton

Beeswax To strengthen and prevent knotting of thread

Scissors Scissors of moderate size and weight should be chosen, sharp with good points. It is a good idea to keep one pair for cutting the fabric. You should have a second pair for cutting the papers. Cutting paper blunts a good pair of scissors. Dressmaking shears are too heavy and clumsy for accurate work

areas. The women from England and the Low Countries who sailed into the unknown took with them not only their meagre possessions but their skills too. The traditional patterns and colours which appear in the work show the country of origin of each family of the settlers. Because of the difficulty and time involved in replenishing supplies, thriftiness in the use of materials was imperative. Long winters were also an important factor in establishing patchwork and quilting as a means of providing warm covers and clothing.

Quilt patterns today frequently appear in American magazines which include full details of materials, yardages and colour schemes as well as templates required. The American girl of yesterday did not regard herself ready for marriage until she had made her 'baker's dozen' of quilts, the last one being the most precious, the marriage quilt.

Hundreds of named designs were evolved and handed down and can be found in illustrations of American patchwork. Some stand for a historic occasion, a family or social event. The American Museum at Claverton Manor, near Bath, England, has a fine display of quilts. While the

3

Thimble This enables you to sew with an even rhythm and prevents the finger becoming sore

Lead pencil A good quality B grade for marking out the fabric patches. Never use a ball point pen or indelible pencil. If you do, permanent stains will result when the work is washed

Paper The choice of paper for cutting out the paper linings over which the fabric patches are made is important. The paper can be any colour but it needs to be a fine and crisp weight equal to a light card. Christmas cards, business reports or brochures are ideal. However, it is as well to test that the ink or dye on the printed card does not smudge

A cork board or pad To enable you to see the design and layout of the patches as they are made, use a flat surface into which pins can easily be pushed. A cork bath mat is ideal for this, or a cork floor tile, a polystyrene ceiling tile or a piece of soft fibre board

Templates Templates are an essential part of patchwork equipment. The paper patterns on which each fabric patch is constructed are cut from them. Machine-made templates of metal alloy or hard plastic are on the market in many geometric shapes of various sizes. They are usually sold in sets for each given

1 Solid and window template

size and shape, a solid with a matching window (figure 1). Templates can also be made at home in firm cardboard or a more lasting material. However, their shape must be accurate, especially on the smaller sizes where errors are more noticeable when the work is put together.

Solid templates represent the size of the finished patch and are the patterns from which, in turn, the paper patterns are cut. Accuracy at this stage is very important.

Window templates are for the selection and marking out of the actual patches on the fabric, allowing an extra 50 mm ($\frac{1}{4}$ in) all round for turnings.

Popular shapes worked in patchwork

The hexagon is a six-sided patch with equal sides and angles. It is the easiest shape to construct and join together when in the honeycomb design. It is therefore ideal for the beginner who will find that it works up neatly on its own or combines well with other shapes (figure 2).

The diamond is slightly more difficult than the hexagon because of its two sharp points. It can be used on its own or, very attractively, with the hexagon.

The pentagon is a five-sided shape with equal sides and equal angles. When joined together to make a three-dimensional shape it will form a cup and is often used for children's play items.

The irregular pentagon is a five-sided shape with two sides twice the length of the other three. It works well with the hexagon and diamond.

The long hexagon or church window is a hexagon that has been so compressed that while the sides are of equal length, its angles are altered. It is an attractive and uncomplicated template from which to work, and can be used alone in a variety of ways. It combines well with several other shapes and groups of shapes: the square, the square and octagon, the square and long diamond, or the square, octagon and

long diamond. This shape is often useful for work in which fullness or flares are required, and is frequently seen in ecclesiastical copes. It can be used with any of the recommended types of fabric.

The square demands more care in producing a true patch than any so far mentioned. All its angles are at 90° so it is important to keep the turnings at each corner neat since they lie parallel to the edge and tend to get in the way when joining the patches up. The square is not as easy for the beginner as the hexagon shape. It can be used singly, with the long hexagon, or octagon, or combined with the long hexagon, octagon and long diamond. It is a good shape for machine patchwork, especially when using leather, suede or vinyl.

The octagon is a delightful shape to work in, but it can only be used when combined with a square. To these two can be added the long hexagon or long hexagon and long diamond.

The long diamond is one of the most difficult shapes to construct and use in patchwork. The extremely fine points demand great precision and the correct type of fabric to make the patches successfully. Firm, fine textured fabrics should be chosen along with strong paper or thin card for linings. The surplus fabric at the fine points can never be completely folded away as in the case of the broader diamond. Eight of these patches joined together form an eight-pointed star, the basis of the Star of Bethlehem design. This shape combines with the square, octagon and long hexagon.

Fabrics

The selection of colour and texture, of the natural and manmade fabrics at our disposal, adds to the charm and fascination of the craft. The need to choose the best materials carefully is not always appreciated. The materials used should always be of a similar weight and thickness, firmly woven to avoid fraying and stretching, but they must crease and seam well. Fabrics should be of similar physical characteristics. Natural and synthetic fabrics should not be mixed, largely because the fibres need different sewing and laundering techniques. Cottons and linen fabrics lend themselves to the shapes and patterns used and have been found to be ideal in texture and weave. They are hardwearing and practical, and are easy to sew and maintain.

Fabrics recommended for patchwork

Cottons Dress prints, poplins, shirtings, chintz, denim, good quality gingham, piqué and needlecord. Soft furnishing fabrics often have interesting surface textures. Fine cottons require a lining such as muslin, fine lawn or Vilene. The latter can be used instead of paper lining and left in place.

Linen Fine linen is excellent and will break up a plain area background. But its weight needs to be watched.

Cotton mixtures such as Viyella are useful additions and wear well in patchwork, but they need more care in preparation as patches as they become bulky when folded.

Pure silk needs extra care in handling and making up. It is suitable for ecclesiastical work and box linings.

Velvet can be combined with silk if it is of a comparable thickness. This gives a very rich finish, but it is not recommended for the inexperienced worker as greater skill is required in constructing patches. A problem is also found when sewing the patches together. The pile can prevent the joining stitch catching into the foundation fabric.

Wool and tweed mixtures come in a wide range of weights, textures and weaves. They are very suitable for handbags or fashion items and are excellent for machine work. Bulky fabrics require extra care in making up. Allow extra width for turnings.

Leather and suede can be used for more experienced work. These materials need no turnings and are very suitable for machine work.

Fabrics difficult to use in patchwork

Cotton-backed vinyl can be used as for leather and suede but it is affected by temperature when working. In cold weather it becomes too firm for easy manipulation.

Rayons and other manmade fabrics can be used but they are very difficult for beginners. Cotton mixed with rayon gives a firm and more durable fabric. Interesting textures can be found in this medium.

Nylon and Terylene and other synthetic fabrics are not considered ideal for patchwork. Their crease resisting nature makes them difficult to fold over papers.

With practice you will find you will recognize a good material and suitable design. Before using any material see that all the pieces are clean and well pressed. When combining new and used fabrics wash the new fabric before use to allow it to shrink, so ensuring that it will not pull against the old when the finished item is subsequently washed.

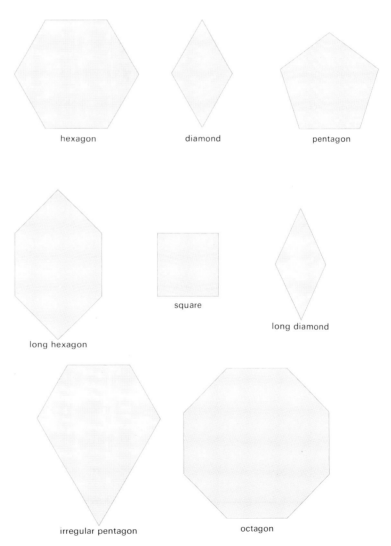

2 *Popular template shapes*

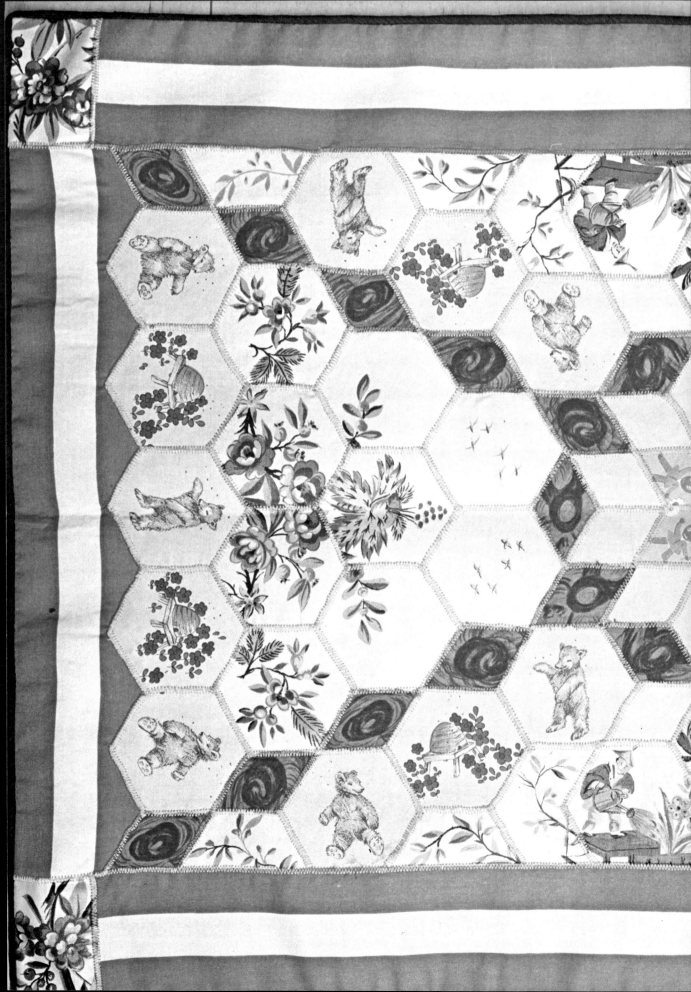

A delicately constructed quilt using blocks of hexagons carefully outlined with diamonds.

Preparation of patches

After the fabrics have been chosen and the template shape and size selected to suit the object you have decided to make, the patches are assembled.

Papers are cut first, using a piece of the firm card. Accuracy at this stage is very important. Errors made now will distort the final piece of work.

Cutting the paper patterns

Place the solid template on the card. Hold firmly between the thumb and the middle finger, cut round the shape with the paper scissors, the blades hugging the metal (figure 3). Make certain that the points are sharp.

This is best done by cutting beyond each point before continuing to the next side. Alternatively, you can draw round the template with a sharp pencil before cutting the paper, although this method is not as accurate. Whichever method is adopted for cutting the paper patterns, it should be practised throughout the piece. This is particularly important on a communal piece of work where many helpers with different degrees of skill may be involved. Two paper patterns may be cut at any one time if the paper is folded, but as accuracy is of prime importance single cutting is recommended.

Cutting the fabric patch

Fabrics are cut by using the window template. The central aperture allows you to choose the portion of material required. The effect of the finished patch can be seen at this stage. After choosing your material, turn it over and lay the template on the wrong side, drawing round the outer edge with a pencil or tailor's chalk. If the pattern does not show through from the wrong side it may be necessary to draw on the right side but this should be avoided because it marks the material. Cut out on the pencil line. A sound principle is to have two sides of the template on the straight of the fabric (figure 4).

Construction of the patches

Place the paper pattern in the centre of the fabric patch on the wrong side of the material. Pin to begin with, but avoid this after practice. Coarse pins leave marks, so do dusty ones. Chintz, glazed and other treated cottons, silks and satins are permanently marked when the surface is broken. Starting with a side on the straight of the fabric (figure 5), tack it over paper. This is done by taking a stitch through the fabric and the paper about one-third of the way along the first side. The second side is then folded over. A tacking stitch is put through the fold

at the corner and brought up one-third of the way along the second side. Continue round the patch, taking a tacking stitch from corner to corner until the patch is complete. It is a mistake to tack too finely. See that the tacking goes through the folds of the first fabric and card but avoid taking the tacking stitch through to the right side. Dirty or coloured cotton will also mark your fabric. Do not use a knot to start with or a back stitch to finish, for this impedes the removal of tacking threads when the work is complete.

As the fabric turnings are made, make sure that their folded edge coincides with the paper beneath and press the fabric well with your fingers. Corners require special attention and pressing if they are to be crisp and true to shape.

Completed patches can either be pinned on to the cork board or kept flat in a shallow box so that you do not crush them.

Joining patches

Using a fine needle and fine sewing cotton, join the patches together by oversewing on the wrong side. Keep the tension of the sewing cotton firm, and with small neat stitches, avoid sewing into the paper linings.

Originally only white and black thread was fine enough for joining patches and so in traditional work only white and black were used.

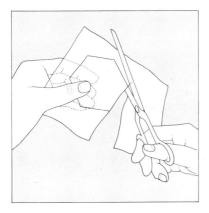

3 Cutting paper from a solid template, showing cut beyond corner

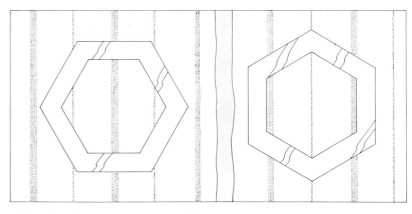

4 Use of window template in cutting fabric

Nowadays modern cotton threads are manufactured in a good range of colours in the same thickness as white and black. Modern work can incorporate other colours. It is recommended that you use a predominant colour as otherwise the work will look bitty.

Take two patches, place the right sides of the fabric together and match the corners exactly. Oversew two sides together, A to B (figure 6), taking care to sew from the beginning of the side to its extreme end. The cotton end is sewn in for about 50 mm ($\frac{1}{4}$ in). Avoid catching the paper. Fasten off securely by oversewing back for 50 mm ($\frac{1}{4}$ in). Open the seam out and press with your thumbs so that the two patches lie flat. On the right side the stitches should not be obtrusive but, if fine and even, they can form part of the design. A third patch is then joined (figure 7). Match the two edges exactly as before and stitch from C to B. The angle of B must fit accurately. Seam from B to D with the same thread.

When working a large piece of patchwork it is helpful to join the patches in strips, straight edge to straight edge, then join the strips to form a piece of fabric. With the aid of the cork board (figure 8) this helps to keep the design in position and makes it possible to join patches with fewer joins in the cotton thread.

Making up the edge of patchwork

The last stage of the work before removing the papers is to fill out the zigzag edge to the required shape of the article. This can easily be done by putting in another patch and turning half of it under (figure 9a). Alternatively, a half or part patch can be made (figure 9b), but this produces a bulkier edge and is not recommended unless the chosen fabric is in short supply. Remember to allow enough work for turnings.

Finishing patches

Having joined all the patches, the next stage is the final make-up of the article. This is irksome to some people and is often approached with a lack of interest. As a result the patchwork becomes limp and lifeless once the paper linings have been removed. A great deal of good work is spoilt at this stage. Try to keep the paper linings in as long as possible. This helps to prevent the work stretching and it is an important point to remember if the patches are being joined together on the bias to form a design, or if one fabric is slightly heavier than the other.

Removal of papers

This is essential for any article that will require laundering and it is the last process before the final finish.

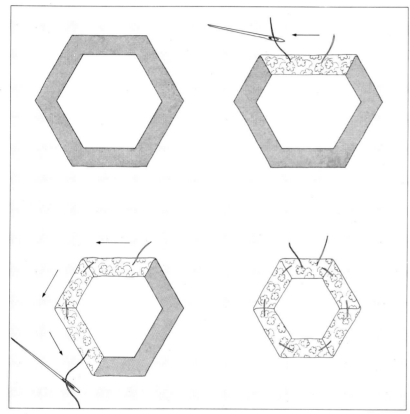

5 *Construction of a patch*

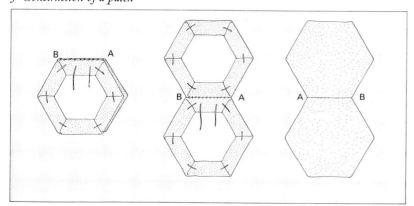

6 *Joining of two patches by oversewing two sides together from A to B*

Remove the tacking threads by putting the scissors under the tacking stitch at X in figure 7 and pulling. The cotton should be removed easily. Press lightly with a warm iron, then remove the papers. By pressing before the papers are removed, the work is not spoilt by the patch turnings showing through on to the top surface. Carefully tack down all the edge turnings to retain the required overall shape. Lay on to the piece of fabric you have chosen for lining or backing the article, wrong sides together.

Linings

These are essential for neatening the back of a piece of patchwork and also help to strengthen the work. They also retain the shape of the article when in use.

Cushions do not require this

A rosette made up of six striped hexagonal patches carefully cut and stitched to form a continuous border round the central red patch.

treatment unless they are made of thin material or fabric that frays easily. A longer life is ensured for a delicate fabric if a lining is fitted.

Dark material will show if the patchwork is in light-coloured fabrics. Suitable fabrics are cambric, lawn and other thin cottons of a weight and colour to match the patches used. For quilts, cotton, linen or unbleached calico combine lightness with strength. The lining of a tea cosy or the back of a cushion cover may be chosen from the same material you have used for some of its patches.

Remember that all linings must be cut on the straight of the fabric

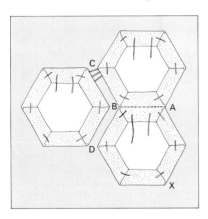

7 Joining of a third patch from C to B and from B to D

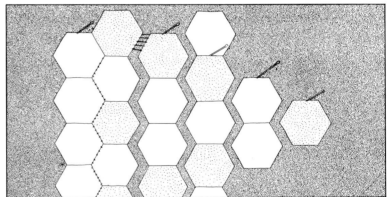

8 Use of cork board to maintain design while working

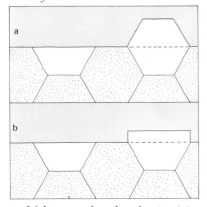

9 Making up edge of work using (a) whole patch and (b) part patch

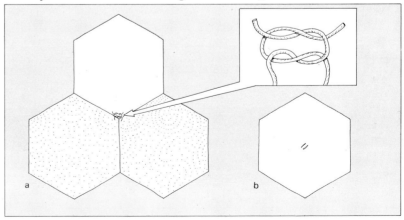

10 Attachment of lining—(a) tying in the centre of a join of patches and (b) tying reef knot in the centre of the patch

you should see that the tie is on the reverse side. Ties which are made on the right side will disappear into the seam.

The first method is stronger, as the thread goes through more layers of material and will not damage a patch.

Cotton threads may very well snap, as they are not strong enough to take the weight of the finished work.

Quilting can be stitched either by hand or by machine, using matching or contrasting cotton. Keep the pattern simple. The design can follow that of the patchwork and the stitching should be the same on the reverse side (figure 11). Whatever method you choose, it is important that attention should be given to the stitch tension.

Embroidery can be used to anchor a piece of patchwork to the lining, at the same time outlining chosen patches or motifs in a simple design. Chain, stem or feather stitch are suitable for this purpose. Spider webs or similar decoration can be used in a dual role, as a focal point in a motif or patch, and as a form of anchorage for the lining.

Finishing techniques

Having completed the piece of patchwork, we need to decide which finishing technique should be used to form the edge of the work and to take the wear.

One of the following can be used.

Quilting edge is the simplest method (figure 12). Turn in the edges of the lining and the patchwork. Tack together, then join by a single or double row of evenly sewn running stitches. Machine stitching can be used, provided the stitch tension is kept even.

Scalloped or patchwork edge is an attractive finish to dress items or a bedcover. This edging often needs to be strengthened by extra lining to give a longer life.

Piping with a cord gives an edge suitable for emphasizing the shape of an article, such as a tea or coffee

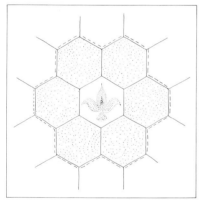

11 Attachment of lining—quilting round the design

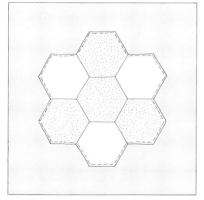

12 Finishing techniques—quilting round outer edge of work

and if the bits you have are small they can be joined to give the necessary size. Where warmth is required, an interlining such as an old blanket, domette, Terylene or cotton wadding can be fitted between the patchwork and the actual lining. There is enough weight, however, in Vilene, Stayflex or stiff card to strengthen a spectacle or needle case.

Attachment of linings

On larger articles such as cot covers, curtains, bedcovers or quilts with a large area of patchwork, the top surface should be attached to the lining, or interlining and lining, to prevent separation and ballooning. This process should not be skimped. It can be done by one of the following methods.

Knotting or tying Using a double piece of linen or buttonhole thread, back stitch through the fabrics twice, tying with a firm reef knot. Knots should be about 22·5 cm (9 in) apart over the work. Stitches can be placed: in the centre of a join of patches or along a join seam (figure 10a); or in the centre of a patch (figure 10b), in which case

pot cosy. It gives a neat, tailored effect and takes the wear, thus protecting the patchwork. Choose a pre-shrunk piping cord of appropriate diameter and length. Cut a bias strip of fabric of a suitable material, 3·5 cm (1½ in) wide, to match the length of the cord. Lay the cord down the middle, on the reverse side, fold it over and stitch close to the cord (figure 13a). Lay the patchwork over the base of the piping, tack and ladder stitch evenly below the cord with a matching cotton (figure 14). Splice the two ends of the piping cord into each other by overlapping the cord ends by 2·5 cm (1 in). Separate the three plies of the cord, leaving one uncut (figure 13b). Cut back the second ply by 1·25 cm (½ in), and the third by 2·5 cm (1 in). Twist the two ends of the cord together and bind firmly with cotton (figure 13c). Hold the

piping cord firmly during this operation. Trim and join the piping fabric to cover the splice as neatly as possible. The position of the join should be anticipated, care being taken to cut the cord and the bias strip to the exact lengths required. To obtain the neatest finish, avoid the piping join coming at the join of two or more patches. Any corners should be squared off. Apply this finish before the work is lined.

Binding is a suitable finish for curtains, skirts or pieces of work that are required to drape. Linings must be put in first, so that both edges are covered in one process. The binding strip should be cut on the bias to the required width, remembering to allow enough material for turnings.

Fringe is an ideal finish to modern style quilts, tablecloths and fashion items of clothing, such as ponchos. Apply the fringe between the

worked surface and the lining, by hand or machine, whichever is most suitable for the work. A handmade fringe can be incorporated to enhance the craftmanship of the work.

Fastenings

Zip fasteners can be used on cushion covers so that the cushion pad can be easily removed for laundering. Cushion pads should be made approximately 2·5 cm (1 in) larger than their covers. Stuff them well to fill out the corners, and plump into shape. Buttons and tags can be made, using patchwork shapes. Join the shapes and stuff with cotton or Terylene wadding, before sewing together.

Hexagons

The hexagon is the simplest grouping of patches, comprising six patches, joined around a central

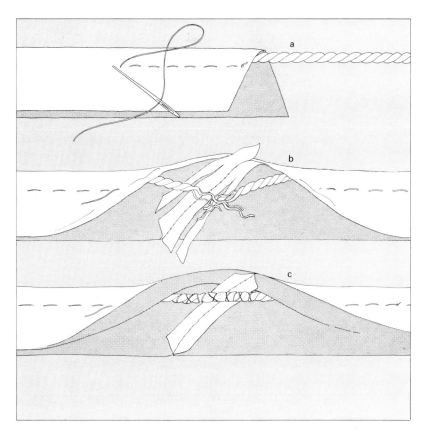

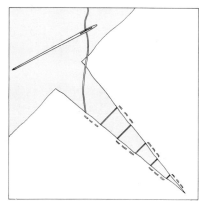

14 Ladder stitch

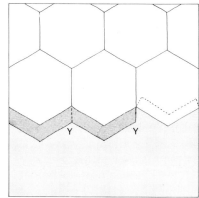

13 Finishing techniques—(a) covering piping cord with bias strip, (b) joining bias strip and cord cut for splicing and (c) spliced join of cord

15 Application of backing to a patchwork edge showing snip at Y

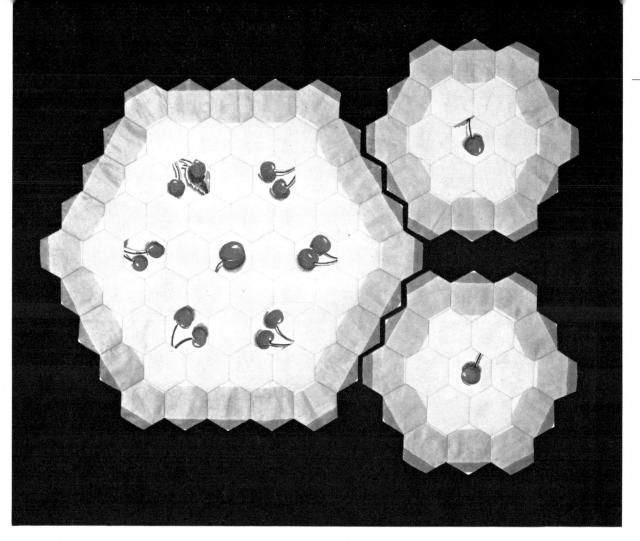

patch. This can be used as a single motif, applied for decoration, or to form a unit in a larger pattern. The way in which patches are grouped, with control of colour and pattern, leads to an overall effect which contrasts pleasingly with a more haphazard arrangement.

Preparation of a seven-patch rosette
Materials required
Scraps of dress cotton, plain and patterned
Set of 2·5 cm (1 in) hexagon templates (solid and window)
Paper
Sewing equipment and cork board
Method
Using the solid template, cut seven papers. Check these for accuracy. Cut seven patches of material, choosing plain and patterned fabrics for effect. Prepare following the method described.

Lay the patches on cork board and build up a design round the central patch. Join the patches together by oversewing on the wrong side.

Set of mats using rosettes of hexagon patches
Materials required
Scraps of cotton fabric, plain and patterned. (Note that a large mat requires 61 patches: 7 motif patches, 30 plain patches, 24 coloured patches. Small mats require 19 patches each: 1 motif patch, 6 plain patches, 12 coloured patches.)
30 cm (12 in) white cotton sheeting to back mats
Set of 1·9 cm ($\frac{3}{4}$ in) hexagon templates
Paper
Sewing equipment and corkboard
Method
Prepare the patches for the first mat as described. Arrange the patches on cork board in position for joining, pinning them at the edges to hold

A set of mats made up of hexagons. By careful measuring and cutting, patterns on a piece of fabric can be cleverly included like these red cherries scattered on a white ground.

them in place (figure 8). Join the patches together in strips, ensuring that the design is correctly positioned. Join the strips together to form one piece of work. Remove the tacking stitches and press lightly before removing the papers. Tack the outer patch turnings to shape. Cut cotton backing material 0·5 cm ($\frac{1}{4}$ in) larger than the finished piece of work. Turn in 0·5 cm ($\frac{1}{4}$ in) and tack, snipping turning at Y (figure 15).

Place the wrong side of the patchwork to the wrong side of the backing and tack into position with small, neat stitches. Oversew the two pieces neatly together. Remove tacking and press lightly. Prepare the small mats in the same manner.

13

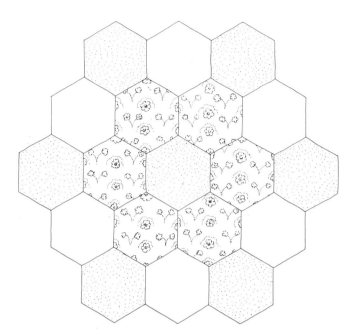

16 *Rosette made up of 19 patches—Grandmother's Flower Garden*

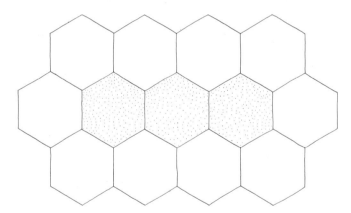

17 *Motif formed from a straight line of patches*

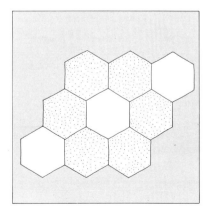

18 *A lozenge motif*

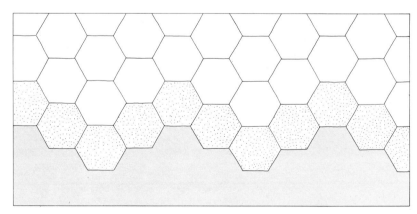

19 *Wavy border design*

Designing with hexagons

The 7-patch rosette can be enlarged by adding 12 patches to form a 19-patch rosette. This shape is the basis for the Grandmother's Flower Garden design so often seen on quilts (figure 16). The rosette shape can be turned into a diamond-shaped block by adding an additional patch on opposite sides. This shape can then be built up by adding patches to form a lozenge (figure 18). Alternatively four, five or more patches can be joined together to form a straight line and a larger motif built up around these (figure 17). Both these motifs can be used with great success on quilts or bed-covers. Very attractive borders can be arranged by joining hexagons in straight strips or in V formations to make a wavy border (figure 19), to a quilt, curtain or long skirt.

Diamonds

The diamond is more difficult to construct than the hexagon because it has two sharply pointed ends. It is, however, a popular shape that can be used in a variety of ways, alone and in combination with other shapes, particularly the hexagon. Three diamonds will form a hexagon, and if each constituent diamond is a different shade they will create the three dimensional box or brick pattern (figure 24). Not all diamonds are of the right proportions to combine with hexagons, and care should be taken to select diamond templates which will combine as this will facilitate both the design and make up of the pattern.

To create a well shaped patch, choose evenly woven, firm cotton or fine linen that will fold and crease well. Good quality silk can be used very successfully once the patch has been mastered in cotton. Treated cottons are not a good medium to begin with, as they tend to be springy in texture. Velvets creep, making a bulky patch, while rayons and other manmade fabrics slip and should therefore be avoided.

Firm paper for the paper patterns is essential to avoid folding at the point of the patch. When cutting the fabric patches, it is advisable to lay one edge of the window template to the thread of the fabric, limiting the natural bias to one direction only (figure 20). This facilitates the folding of the patch and gives a smoother finish to the final article. Work towards a sharp point when constructing the patch, so that the mitred points are prepared neatly and at the same time tacked securely.

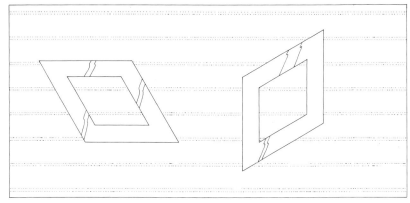

20 Use of diamond window when cutting fabric patch

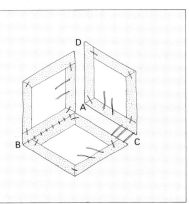

22 Finished diamond patch

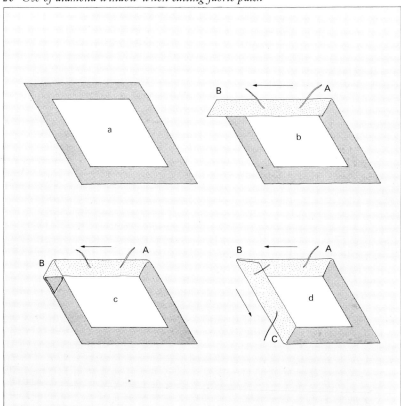

21 Construction of a diamond patch; (a) paper placed on wrong side of fabric;
(b) fabric folded from A to B and tacked; (c) parallel fold at B; (d) fold B to C

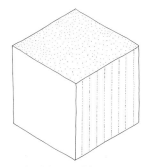

23 Construction of diamond box by joining A to B, C to A then A to D

24 Finished diamond box

15

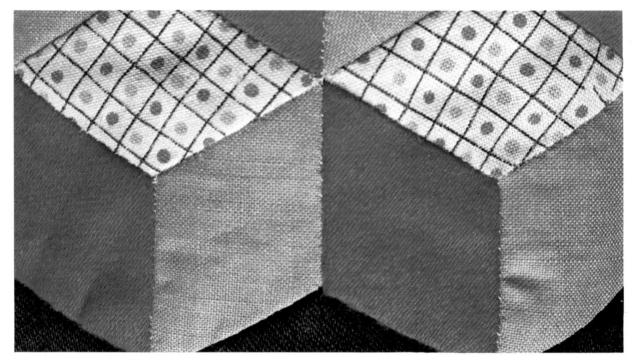

Construction of a diamond patch

Using solid and window templates as for the hexagon, cut paper pattern and fabric patches. Place the paper on the wrong side of the fabric patch (figure 21a). Fold fabric from A to B. Tack (figure 21b). Fold fabric at point B so that the fold runs parallel to the edge of the paper, but does not overlap it (figure 21c). Do not stitch this fold. Fold from B to C (figure 21d). Tack. Continue as for the hexagon, repeating the fold at D. Avoid taking the tacking stitch through to the right side of the patch. It can be helpful to practise first, using a patch cut from thin paper instead of fabric. When the technique is mastered, prepare three fabric patches, making certain they are all true to shape (figure 22). Join them to form a box or brick pattern (figure 24).

Construction of a diamond box

Take two of the prepared diamonds and with the right side of fabric together, match the two sharp points. Oversew from A to B.

A clever three-dimensional effect is created by blocks of diamond patches joined to form this cover for a Denbyware coffee jug.

Attach a third patch by joining from C to A, and from A to D (figure 23).

Cover for a 750 ml (1½ pt) Denbyware coffee jug

Materials required

Selection of cotton fabrics to give light, medium and dark tones

Set of 2·5 cm (1 in) diamond templates

0·25 x 1 m (12 x 40 in) material for lining

Cotton wool

Paper

Sewing equipment and cork board

(The cover is made up from a body, top and knob)

Method

Prepare 41 box patches, using the three diamond shapes described.

Body of cover Arrange 40 of these boxes on cork board, in four rows of ten to form a rectangle. Join up boxes in horizontal strips. Join the four strips together to form a rectangle, which should be checked

to ensure it fits over the jug. Remove the tacking from the patchwork patches and press lightly. Remove the papers from the patches and tack around outer edge to hold them in shape.

Cut the lining material to 45 x 21 cm (18 x 8¼ in) (figure 25). Fold in and tack the turnings to give a rectangle of 45 x 17 cm (18 x 6¾ in). Place the patchwork over the lining which has been cut to shape. Tack firmly into position. Ladder stitch

16

neatly (figure 14). Slip stitch the short sides of the lining together. Finally join the patchwork shapes together, using ladder stitch.

Top of cover Cut two circles 17 cm (6¾ in) in diameter from lining material. Turn in 1 cm (⅜ in) round both circles and tack them, wrong sides together, to form the top of the cosy. Find the centre of the top and apply the remaining box patch, having removed the papers.

Making the knob Prepare three smaller diamond patches, approximately 2 cm (¾ in), in lining material. Join them together, leaving one side open. Stuff with cotton wool, making certain the points are well filled. Close the seam and attach very securely to the centre of the box patch, taking the stitches through to the lining to prevent ballooning. Having attached the knob, oversew the circle to one end of the patchwork cylinder to complete the cover.

Variations on the use of the diamond shape

Trellis pattern is a combination of diamonds joined in an upright position giving a trellis, or leaded window effect and can be used as a border for fashion items and quilts (figure 26).

Zigzag pattern makes an effective border or edge obtained by joining diamonds together in this way (figure 27).

Six-pointed star is an attractive design, built up from diamond shapes, that can be used in articles of all sizes, from a small pincushion to a much larger item, where it combines very well with the hexagon or is itself enlarged to form a hexagon shape, by the addition of six diamond patches (figure 28).

Construction of a six-pointed diamond star
Materials required
Scraps of dress cotton, plain and patterned
A set of diamond templates
Paper

Sewing equipment and cork board
Method
Prepare six diamond patches. Attach them to the cork board to develop the contrasting effect of the plain and patterned fabrics. Take two of the prepared patches and with the right sides of the fabric together, match the two sharp points and oversew from A to B.

Attach a third patch in the same manner and join from C to B (figure 29). Assemble another three patches in the same way. Join the two sets together from D to E. Joining the patches in this way, enables the points at the centre to fit well without a hole. When complete, the star should be lying absolutely flat.

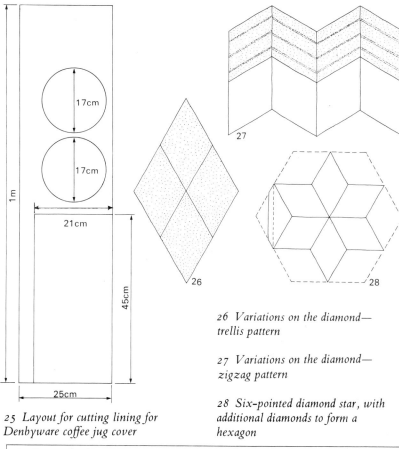

26 *Variations on the diamond—trellis pattern*

27 *Variations on the diamond—zigzag pattern*

28 *Six-pointed diamond star, with additional diamonds to form a hexagon*

25 *Layout for cutting lining for Denbyware coffee jug cover*

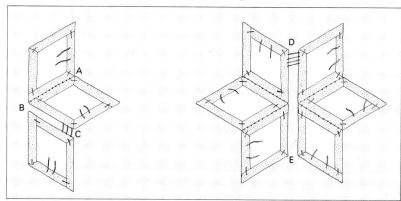

29 *Procedure for assembling six-pointed diamond star*

17

Combinations using diamond and hexagon shapes

1 A rosette formed by surrounding one hexagon with a ring of six diamond boxes (figure 30)

2 A rosette formed by surrounding a diamond box by six hexagons (figure 31)

3 Strips of hexagons connected by fitting in single diamonds (figure 32)

4 Straight or diagonal strips of hexagons connected with diamond boxes (figure 33)

5 A six-point star surrounded by hexagons with a further ring of six-point stars (figure 34)

Chair cushion using six-point stars and hexagons

Material required for cushion to fit a Windsor chair

Scraps of cotton materials, floral patterns for the hexagon patches, plain or small mixture design for the diamond patches

50 cm (20 in) cotton material for backing and ties, or a piece of fabric similar to the patches

Piece of cotton or Terylene wadding, 40 x 40 cm (16 x 16 in)

125 cm (50 in) cotton piping cord

Set of 2·5 cm (1 in) diamond templates

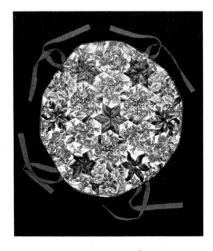

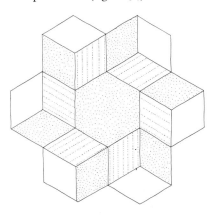

30 Hexagon surrounded by six box patches

31 Rosette from a box patch surrounded by six hexagonal patches

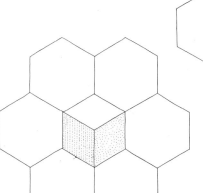

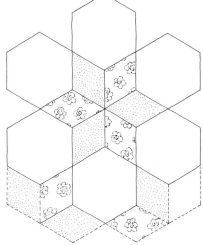

33 Diagonal strips of hexagons joined by diamond boxes

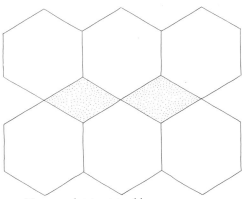

32 Hexagonal strips joined by diamonds

34 Six-pointed star surrounded by hexagons to connect further stars

Set of 2·5 cm (1 in) hexagon templates
Paper
Sewing equipment and cork board

Method

Make a paper pattern of the chair seat and attach it to the cork board. Following the layout of the cushion illustrated, you will need to make up:

7 six-pointed diamond star motifs (42 diamond patches)

12 diamond patches to connect star and hexagon shapes

48 hexagons

Having arranged star motifs and patches, join them together until the work fills the required area. Add further patches if required. Remove outer round of papers and fold in overhang. Tack work to the shape required. Prepare piping cord as directed. Use backing material for the bias strip (figure 35). Tack piping cord. Attach using ladder stitch with matching cotton, joining the piping cord by splicing. Remove tacking from the other patches, press lightly and remove papers. Cut the backing material to the paper shape, allowing 1 cm ($\frac{1}{2}$ in) for turnings. Fold in turnings and tack to shape. Cut cotton or Terylene wadding to shape and lay between patchwork and backing. Attach the interlining and backing to the front, by knotting through from the centre of three hexagon patches. Prepare four ties. Cut eight pieces of backing material 3 x 25 cm ($1\frac{1}{4}$ x 10 in). Fold in half, right sides together, join, and open to the right side. Press. Position ties to attach round the legs of the chair, allowing at least 1 cm ($\frac{1}{2}$ in) insertion to secure within the cushion. Tack and sew in place. Tack backing to piped edge and ladder stitch neatly. Remove tacking stitches and give a final press to the finished cushion.

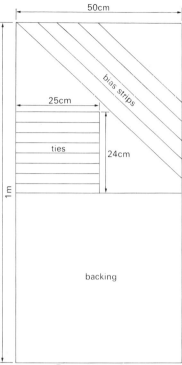

35 *Layout for cutting cushion backing, ties and bias strip*

A floral chair cushion cover made up of diamonds and hexagons with laces for attaching to the chair legs.

Pentagons

The five-sided shape most often seen is the equilateral pentagon, which has equal angles and sides. Unlike the hexagon, a rosette of pentagons can never lie flat and must form a cup-shaped and three-dimensional body. Toy makers use this cup shape to make soft balls, joined together with ladder stitch (figures 38, 39) to create Christmas tree decorations, simple dolls and animals such as Charlie the Caterpillar.

Construction of a pentagon rosette or cup

Materials required
Scraps of cotton or linen fabric
2·5 cm (1 in) pentagon template
Paper
Sewing equipment

Method
Prepare six pentagon patches, using the same method as for hexagons. Oversew patches together (figure 36). Join two patches from A to B. Taking a third patch, join from C to B, then from B to D. Continue inserting the remaining patches in the same way, until you reach A. Close up from A to J (figure 37).

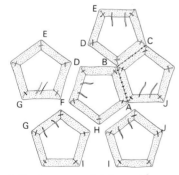

36 Pentagon cup, joining patches

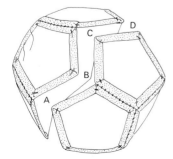

38 Joining two pentagon cups

Variations on a pentagon ball

Christmas tree decorations made up of pentagon balls can be prepared from scraps of lurex or brocade fabrics, tacked over firm card, which is retained in the finished ball. These balls hang from a piece of ribbon or cord, attached to one side, and then can be decorated with beads and/or sequins.

Embroidery embellished felt ball Design twelve simple motifs to fit into the chosen patch size, and transfer to the felt. Work the designs before cutting out with contrasting embroidery threads. Use a variety of stitches, such as chain stitch, detached chain stitch, whipped chain or whipped stem stitch, or fly stitch. Cut out the felt shape with the metal template. Care is needed to get each patch identical. Join patches as for the ball, but stitch on the right side. Using embroidery cotton, stitch together from right to left, then repeat from left to right, so forming cross stitches. Variation to this could be a buttonhole stitch.

Character dolls A large and a small pentagon ball will create a chubby doll. Appropriate colours and mat-

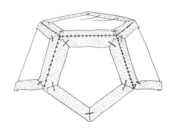

37 Finished pentagon cup

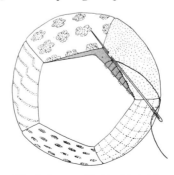

39 Final closure of ball with ladder stitch

erials can be selected for the different patches to represent hair, flesh and costume. Features can be portrayed by embroidery and appliqué. Feet and arms can then be added if desired.

Charlie the caterpillar

The caterpillar brings into use a range of patchwork balls of different sizes. The head is made from the largest ball, each ball thereafter being a size smaller. By joining the balls with press studs, the caterpillar can be made to grow larger or shorter as required. Velcro can be used as an alternative to press studs.

Materials required
Strong cotton or linen fabric in greens and yellowish browns
Pentagon templates 3·7, 3·1, 2·8, 2·5, 2·1, 1·8, 1·5, 1·2 cm ($1\frac{1}{2}$, $1\frac{1}{4}$, $1\frac{1}{8}$, 1, $\frac{7}{8}$, $\frac{3}{4}$, $\frac{5}{8}$, $\frac{1}{2}$ in)
7 press studs
Washable toy filling
Vilene
Paper
Sewing equipment and cork board

Method
Use green patterned material for each top cup and yellowish brown for each lower cup.

Head of caterpillar Prepare twelve 3·7 cm ($1\frac{1}{2}$ in) pentagons, two plain green ones on which the eyes are embroidered, four patterned green ones and six yellowish brown ones. One of the four patterned green patches should be made over Vilene which will hold a press stud firmly. Make up the ball, remove the papers, but not the Vilene, and reverse the work. Sew one half of a press stud firmly on the Vilene-backed patch, working right through the fabrics. Stuff firmly and ladder stitch the final opening. Embroider eyes in the centre of the plain green patches, with a mouth slightly below.

Body Make up seven more balls using the other templates in turn. A Vilene backed patch will be required at the front and back of each of these balls, except for the smallest, which will not need one at the back where there is no press stud. Con-

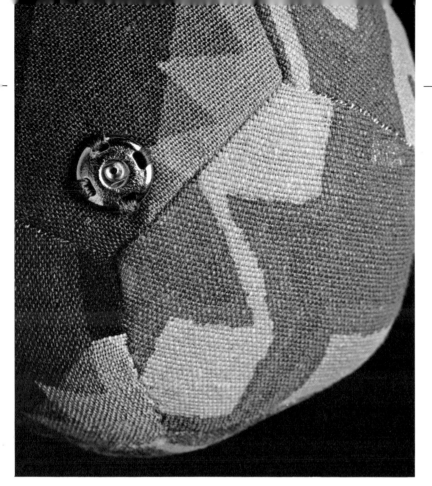

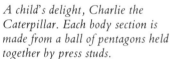

A child's delight, Charlie the Caterpillar. Each body section is made from a ball of pentagons held together by press studs.

sult the illustration when planning the layout of the patches and the position of press studs. Snap balls together.

Machine patchwork

The sewing techniques adopted with the advent of the sewing machine in the last century were soon applied to the preparation and assembly of patchwork. As the sewing machine became more sophisticated, so it became possible to adapt it to creative patchwork. Shapes, however, must be simple. Squares and rectangles being especially suitable if you are working with patches of 3·5 cm (1½ in) and over in length. As with handwork, accuracy in cutting and stitching the patches together is essential if a good result is to be obtained.

The swing needle machine has made machine patchwork a speedy alternative to hand sewing, although

not as relaxing for the worker. It saves time when producing fashion items and is a suitable technique for modern fabrics which require no turnings. The zigzag stitch is invaluable in decorative stitchery, but extravagant with thread. Be sure you have a sufficient supply of the required colour before commencing an article.

When using machine patchwork for an item of clothing, choose a simple pattern. Some shapes take darts more kindly than others. It helps when designing to draw out-

lines of patches on to a paper pattern, noting where darts or seams occur. Many fabrics can be used for machine work, particularly cottons, needlecords, wools and fine tweeds, silks and velvets. Leather, suede and vinyl are particularly good as they will not fray and therefore do not require turnings. Densely woven fabrics are likely to be too bulky for the machine needle mechanism.

Handling of the machine

Care is necessary to maintain an even stitch tension. Use the correct thread for the weight and type of fabric being worked. Always check with folded scraps of fabric similar to that in the work before you commence. It is important to maintain the same type and colour of thread throughout the work. Remember to change the needle when it becomes blunt, otherwise the fabric will be marred. Ensure that the machine is regularly cleaned and is running smoothly. The precise nature of patchwork will reflect any uneven running due to flick, dust or wear.

Straight stitchwork

This is simple machine patchwork that does not involve the use of templates. It can be made up from strips of varying widths seamed together, with an allowance to form a larger striped piece. Open out the turnings and press them flat. Prepare other strips in the same manner. Trim strips to size and join all together to form a piece of fabric large enough for the required article. This is a very simple method of machine work and ideal for preparing curtains or colourful cotton or wool skirts.

Squares and rectangles can also be joined in this way. First, cut patches by marking round a template with a pencil on the reverse side of the fabric. Cut out patches, leaving 1 cm (½ in) for turnings. Arrange patches to the required design, then join them together in strips along the pencil lines. Press each seam flat before joining to other strips.

Patches can also be joined by turning in a seam allowance, then overlapping the patches to form the design, stitching from the right side. Irregular shapes can be joined in this way, overlapping and stitching, piece by piece.

Swing needle work

For this type of work patches should be cut exactly to the template, then placed in position on a cotton or calico backing and held at the corners with a fine pin. It is advisable to stitch a row at a time, joining with a zigzag stitch, and finish by securing the threads firmly at the back with a double reef knot. Cotton patches can be backed with an iron-on material and the joins covered with a wide zigzag stitch. The patches should just overlap by about 3 mm ($\frac{1}{8}$ in). Work prepared in this way is better washed before being made up, to reduce stiffness. Hexagon and diamond shapes can be joined in this manner, using dress or fine furnishing cottons that do not fray. Thought should be given to the stitching so that unnecessary joins are avoided.

Diamonds and hexagons using a swing needle

Cut the patches exactly to the size of the template to be used. Lay the patches on the iron-on interlining. Pin them in position. Iron the patches to the interlining with a warm iron, using the point of the iron. Avoid the base of the iron touching any of the interlining or it will become sticky. Work methodically until all the patches are in position.

Set the sewing machine to a wide swing at about 30-35 stitches per 2·5 cm/1 in. Diamonds are easily stitched together in lines. Ensure at each junction that the next pair of patch edges is centred under the swing needle. It is more important to catch all the patch edges than to have ruler straight lines. Joining hexagons is more complicated. The angle of the needle must be changed at each patch junction. On every fourth hexagon angle, the stitching will overlap. Reduce the stitch width to a narrow one and make a stitch line parallel to the original one. Widen the stitch width before stitching the next section. This method reduces the number of joins in a piece of work. It is known as the Coscote method and was developed by Mrs Julia Roberts of Didcot (figure 40).

A closer look reveals the machine overstitching around each patch worked with a swing needle machine.

Log cabin patchwork

Log cabin is an early form of block patchwork. Each block is composed of narrow strips of overlapping fabric built out from a central square. The ends of the strips overlap representing the log structure of the cabins of early American settlers. On the American continent, this type of patchwork has enjoyed a continuous popularity. Some of the traditional arrangements of the patterned squares have interesting symbolic titles such as 'Barn Raising', 'Straight Furrow', 'Goose Flight' and 'Windmill'. In one example, light and dark patches occupy two

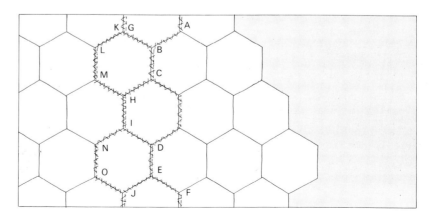

40 Method of joining hexagons with zigzag stitch

adjacent sides respectively of a block. It is said that the central square represents the fire, and the light half of the block, the firelit side of a room. The dark side represents its shadow.

In the UK, log cabin patchwork was worked in tweed and woollen scraps to make warm bed coverings. In later years, the woollen fabrics were superseded by printed cottons, velvets and silks. Coloured ribbons were also used to give an effect of different timbers, and sometimes a whole quilt was made up from ribbons, using to advantage the different textures.

The blocks of patchwork will vary in size depending on the article required. A 30-38 cm (12-15 in) block is usual for a bedcover and a 15 cm (6 in) block for smaller items, such as a cushion or a handbag. One essential aspect of block patchwork is the concealment of the stitchery by the careful use of reverse sewn turnings. In addition to the use of foundation material to form the blocks, a backing is required to neaten the final work.

The log cabin method is very suitable for machine work and can be done with or without foundation material. If no foundation material is used, very firm and even-weight fabrics should be selected for the patches.

Although the log cabin is made up with templates, none are manufactured, as each object requires a

fresh set to suit its own block size. The size of the object determines the size of its constituent blocks which in turn decides the size of the square and the patches to be used in the block. A template should be cut from stiff, good quality card, around which the squares of foundation material can be cut. The template is also ruled to show the design within the block, and so the size of the strips can be calculated accurately.

The squares of foundation material are cut, using the template, from firm, fine cotton to give ease of sewing. The surface fabric is marked out into strips on the wrong side with a pencil and ruler. The pencil line should outline the finished patch size as a guide for straight stitching, either by hand or machine. The strips should be cut 5 mm ($\frac{1}{4}$ in) wider on both sides allowing for the turnings.

To prepare a log cabin block
Materials required
Piece of fine cotton or lawn for foundation square
Long scraps of dress cotton, light and dark tones
Card for templates
Pencil and ruler
Sewing equipment
Method
Cut out and mark a template for the foundation material, 15 cm (6 in) square (figure 41). Cut out a template for the centre square, 3·5 cm

($1\frac{3}{8}$ in), which will give a patch approximately 2 cm ($\frac{3}{4}$ in) square. Using the larger templates, cut out the foundation material. Make crease marks along the diagonal from each corner, so that they cross in the centre (figure 42). This can be done with tacking thread. It will give the position for the central square. Using the small template, cut out the square patch to be used in the centre (figure 43). Position on the crossing diagonals and stitch in place. Cut up the long scraps of dress material into 3 cm ($1\frac{1}{4}$ in) strips, allowing for turning widths on both sides. Cut each strip into patches so that each one is longer, by one width, than the one before, thus creating the log cabin effect. Where several blocks are to be used, each block is built up in either a clockwise or anti-clockwise direction. Care should be taken to see that all blocks are built up in the same direction, or as the overall pattern dictates. Select your patch material to give the desired light and dark effect. If you do not wish to cut up your patches in advance, long strips of fabric can be prepared and measured, then cut as the work progresses.

The shortest strip of the material is first pinned along one side of the seam allowance of the centre square, then sewn 5 mm ($\frac{1}{4}$ in) from the edge (figure 44). Use running stitches in a strong cotton, with an

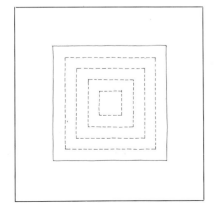

41 Marking foundation template

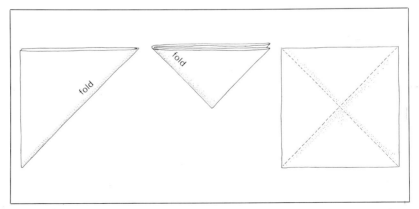

42 Folding and tacking foundation material to mark centre

occasional back stitch for extra firmness. Fold the patch material back over the stitches and press down. The next longest strip of material is pinned and sewn along the second side of the centre square. This time, however, overlap the end of the first strip (figure 45). The third and fourth strips are then added in the same way, until all the sides of the centre square are covered, remembering to overlap the previous strip (figures 46, 47). The process is repeated on the next round, the seam allowance of the first row of strips being covered. The process is repeated for each round. The final round of strips is folded over so that it meets the edges of the foundation (figure 48). Tack the edge of the outer round to the foundation. An alternative method of building up the pattern is shown in figure 49.

To make a purse or make-up bag

An interesting small, useful article can be quickly assembled from two log cabin blocks. The blocks are joined together and lined, using the technique in the following section. Oversew the two side seams and insert a zip fastener.

Method of joining blocks

Position the blocks for the required design and place two together with right sides facing. Pin and tack accurately. Stitch firmly with back stitches, allowing a generous seam of 1 cm ($\frac{1}{2}$ in) (figure 50). Open the seam and press it. Continue joining the other blocks until they form a piece of work. Tack the lining in position, anchored at intervals to prevent ballooning and finish with a quilting edge or a piping cord.

Two other variations of log cabin

The pineapple pattern is made up on the same principles as the log cabin. On alternate rounds, however, the strips around the centre square are placed across the corners diagonally (figure 51). Rounds worked in two colours, one light and the other dark, give an attractive three-dimensional effect.

The Vee pattern is a traditional method used in the North of England and Wales to provide a decorative border on old strip quilts. Patches of coloured material are laid diagonally on to a narrow foundation strip (figure 52). These are stitched and folded in the same way as log cabin. A second strip is prepared with the patches arranged on the opposite diagonal. The two strips are then tacked together and

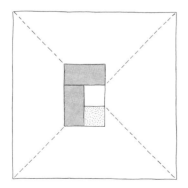

43 Log cabin—positioning and stitching centre patch

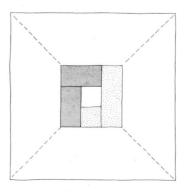

44 Log cabin—stitching first strip to centre patch

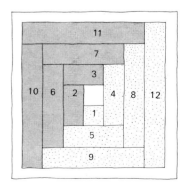

45 Log cabin—stitching second strip to centre patch, overlapping first strip

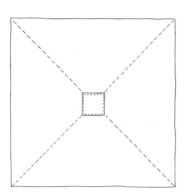

46 Log cabin—third strip stitched in position

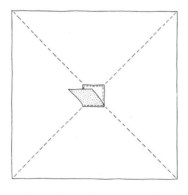

47 Log cabin—fourth strip in position

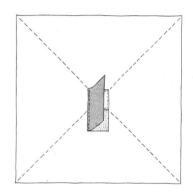

48 Log cabin—completed block

seamed down the centre, taking care to match patches.

Log cabin cushion cover

In this project, we are going to build a single central square from four log cabin blocks, with dominant linking strips. This central square is surrounded by three rounds of log cabin strips to complete the overall design.

Material required

Quantity of various cotton fabrics, patterned and plain in light, medium and dark tones, with 70 cm (27½ in) of bold, dominant colour to form the centre cross

Fine cotton fabric for foundation, 60 cm x 1 m (24 x 36 in)

Template 2.5 x 2.5 cm (1 x 1 in)

Template 11.5 x 11.5 cm (4½ x 4½ in)

Template 27 x 27 cm (10½ x 10½ in)

2 m (2 yd) piping cord, pre-shrunk

30 cm (12 in) zip fastener
Ruler
Sewing equipment

Method

Front of cushion cover The central square should be prepared from four log cabin blocks 11.5 cm (4½ in) square with centre squares of

A brilliant orange cross divides four log cabin blocks. The log cabin, a unique construction of strips of varying length, is one of the great traditional designs of North America.

2.5 cm (1 in) cut from the dominant fabric, and four rounds of strips 2.5 cm (1 in) wide. Arrange the fabrics as illustrated. The linking strips should be cut from two strips of the dominant fabric, 5 x 12.5 cm (2 x 4½ in). Join two blocks together with one of these strips, along a dark edge. Repeat with the second strip, joining the two remaining blocks. Press open all seams. Cut a third strip in the dominant fabric 5 x 27 cm (2 x 10½ in). Join the two linked blocks with this strip. Press seams open.

The outer pattern Position the central square on a piece of foundation material 50 cm (19½ in) square, using the diagonal technique to find a centre point. Cut strips of fabric in light, medium and dark colours, 5 cm (2 in) wide to run round the edge of the central square. Join these to the central square, working one round in light, one in medium, and one in dark coloured strips. Tack outer round to the foundation. Turn in edges 1.25 cm (½ in) and tack.

Back of cushion cover Prepare a large single log cabin block with a central square 27 cm (10½ in), preferably of similar fabric or colour to one of the fabrics in the small blocks on the front piece of the work. Stitch to centre of the foundation square, 50 cm (19½ in). Cut strips of fabric, light, medium and dark, 5 cm (2 in) wide, similar to the outer strips on the front work. Join these to form a block as for the front. Tack the outer round to the foundation. Turn in edges 1.25 cm (½ in) and tack. Cover piping cord with a bias strip using material as central patch if possible. Attach piping cord to both sides, inserting zip fastener as required.

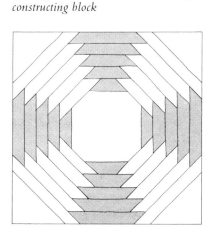

49 Log cabin—alternative method of constructing block

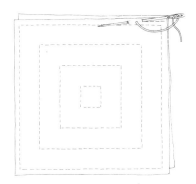

50 Log cabin—method of joining two blocks together

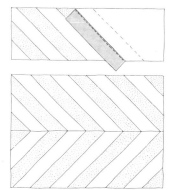

51 The pineapple pattern

52 The Vee pattern—(a) stitching diagonal patches to foundation material; (b) joining strips of diagonal patches

Patchwork quilts

The ambition of most needle-women, having mastered patch-work techniques is to produce a quilt or bedcover which will become a family heirloom. A piece of special work, which will be handed down from generation to generation, like so many family quilts. A well made quilt is a thing of beauty, requiring time and patience in its preparation, so it must be durable. Always use new material. This is the most important thing to remember if the quilt is to last. The material can be sewing scraps, dressmaking or furnishing leftovers, pieces with a sentimental value, or fabric purchased specially to tone in.

Traditionally, the best patchwork quilts were made with a design plan that was repeated over the entire top. Patchwork quilts without a repeat plan have always been made and used as everyday quilts. They were made up from dressmaking scraps and usable portions of old clothes. The design was dictated by the choice of fabric as it came to hand. Irregular patterns were created from a combination of squares, triangles and stripes.

The difference between irregular design quilts and crazy quilts lies in the way in which they are sewn. Irregular designs are patchwork shapes pieced together to form the quilt top. Crazy quilts are made of irregularly shaped pieces of fabric, appliquéd or laid on to a single, large piece of backing.

Constructing the block pattern quilt is simple and has the virtue of covering the ground effectively, with a relatively small amount of work. One way of working out the design for a block pattern is to take a piece of plain paper, the size of the basic block to be used. Fold the square of paper into four sections, open out and use the squares formed by the creases as your templates. The pattern created by the use of chosen materials is then repeated, block by block. Common divisions of a block are into four squares,

known as a four-patch; nine squares, known as a nine-patch; and sixteen squares, known as a sixteen-patch. Blocks are made separately and put aside until they are all finished. They may then be put together in a variety of ways, next to one another, alternating with plain blocks or with lattice strips. Much American work has developed on these lines carrying titles such as 'Jacob's Ladder', 'Road to Oklahoma', 'Wild Goose Chase' and 'Pin Wheels'.

Block designs may be joined by hand or machine. If joined by hand, a running stitch is used with an occasional back stitch for strength. But you must make sure to finish off securely to avoid threads pulling out. If work is produced over papers to form a block design, join by over-sewing. This method gives a firmer, stronger finish. Today many block quilts are joined by machine stitch-ing. Whichever method of joining is used, it is important that all seaming is uniform, as nothing is worse than squares or blocks that do

not join up evenly.

An all over design has one pattern shape or motif, which repeats over and over again. Shapes such as squares, rectangles, hexagons, dia-monds and long hexagons are pieced together in a design that results from the planned position of different coloured or patterned fabrics. Quilts can be multi-coloured or contain a limited amount of colour, depend-ing on the overall design for effect. Many early quilts were made in two colours only, such as red and white, or blue and white. Designs can be created by placing the brightest or darkest pieces so that they stand out to form a pattern. An allover design is a good choice for a charming, but uncomplicated quilt. The plan can be simple and construction can develop from blocks or shapes, such as 'Grandmother's Garden', or 'Loz-enge', linked overall by patches of contrasting or toning colour.

Centre motif quilts have a design beginning from a central point, radiating outwards like 'Stars and

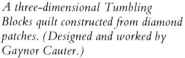

A three-dimensional Tumbling Blocks quilt constructed from diamond patches. (Designed and worked by Gaynor Cauter.)

Sunbursts'. The 'Star of Bethlehem' is an old pattern built up with the long diamond. It requires careful planning at every stage, from the exact construction of each patch, to the total blending of colours radiating from the centre of the pattern.

Commemorative quilts are a form of centre motif. During the nineteenth century, printed central panels or embroidered medallions were specially prepared to celebrate important events. The chosen piece would be surrounded with decorative frames or borders, to make an entire quilt. Today, combinations of embroidery and patchwork have been revived using this interesting and creative approach.

Friendship quilts are usually group projects worked to mark a special occasion such as a marriage, a birth or to commemorate an important event. The constituent blocks were laid out and sewn by different people, then joined together. A very fine modern example is in the American Museum at Bath. It depicts the floral emblems of the thirteen original states of America with those of Great Britain. It was completed in 1976.

Today the easiest way to work out a design and determine which shapes are required, is to plan the work on isometric graph paper, which is obtainable from good stationers. Hexagons, diamonds, irregular pentagons and triangles can be drawn using the printed lines as a guide. Having outlined the required shapes, the colour contrast and the three-dimensional effects, such as diamond boxes, can be shown by pencil shading (figure 53).

Mixing textures is a good way of adding interest to a simple design or colour scheme. The difference in texture produces a slight variation in shade or tone. This can also be achieved by using the material reversed or turned at an angle. A good design can be ruined by failing to make use of natural texture, as well as the pattern of the material. It is at this stage that time spent laying out the patches on the cork board will show in the finished quilt.

Quilting—so rich, so satisfying . . .

Quilting is an ancient craft. The word quilt itself is derived from the latin *culcita* or *culcitra*, meaning a mattress or pillow. *The Concise Oxford English Dictionary* defines it as a bedcover made of padding enclosed between two layers of linen, kept in place by crossed lines of stitching.

The quilting process has been known and practised widely from early times in most European and eastern countries as well as in the Mohammedan regions of Africa. Quilted items have been mentioned in many old documents and household inventories.

The earliest use of quilting was utilitarian, for warmth and protection. In medieval times it was adapted for body armour and knights and foot soldiers often wore quilted jackets under armour and chain mail to prevent chafing. The workmanship was simple as the thickness of the padding and the coarse linen that was used made fine stitchery impossible.

In the Tudor period, decorative quilting appeared on fashionable clothing including nightcaps, waistcoats, doublets, dresses and petticoats made in silk, with floral and other intricate patterns. In the reigns of Queen Anne, George I and George II, as new materials became available they were enriched by the addition of silk embroidery, making them even more elaborate.

Linen quilting using the stuffed method was worked on petticoats, stomachers, pockets and household furnishings. Bed quilts were made with matching bed hangings and cushions. They were easy to launder and had a long life.

By the end of the Regency period, new fabrics and a fundamental change in fashion led to the decline in popularity of quilted clothing. Quilts and bedcovers however continued as important household items, many being made by professional quilters as well as by housewives. In the nineteenth century the expanding textile industry produced machine made quilts of various kinds. One known as the Marseilles or Marcella quilt was woven so ingeniously that it copied the raised effect of the quilting process. Manufactured quilts were cheaper and more plentiful and while not as warm as handmade ones, they became very popular.

During Queen Victoria's reign the introduction of both inexpensive machine made blankets and fashionable eiderdowns reduced the use of bed quilts. In many homes quilting continued, but it was only in Durham and Wales that the use of the true traditional quilting patterns was maintained through to the present day.

Patchwork uses many of the same techniques as quilting and the two art forms have often been used together. The basic designs used in patchwork will be found in quilting, although in the latter additional sewn embellishment is added to enrich it.

Equipment

Work basket essential items include:
Needles No. 7-10 Betweens, small fine needles for English quilting. A rug or yarn needle for marking patterns on to the fabric.
Tailor's chalk can serve as an alternative for marking the design, but it will rub off and not be as permanent as a needle mark
Scissors Two pairs, sharp and of good quality, one pair to cut the fabric and a smaller pair for cutting the threads
Thimble An essential item, which should fit well and feel comfortable. Some quilters also wear a finger shield on the other hand to protect the fingers against continuous pricking, which can be very annoying as well as painful.
Threads of matching pure silk or strong cotton, depending on the fabric used. It should always be thick enough to cover any marking lines. When working an item such as a reversible two coloured quilt, it is usual to use a thread which matches the top side.

Card for the basic templates
Pencil such as a good quality B grade, for marking out the template shapes on the card
Stanley knife for cutting out the templates
Long ruler, yardstick 1m (1 yd) or T square for measuring and marking straight lines
White tape to attach materials to the frame stretchers
Safety pins to attach tape to the materials

Quilting frame

Quilting mounted on a frame makes it easier to achieve even stitchery and ensures that the materials used do not pucker. It allows for greater comfort in working, both hands being free. One hand works on the upper side and the other on the underside of the work. For small pieces of work, use an adjustable embroidery frame. One on a stand is preferable to a hoop frame, as it does not distort the work and enables it to be tilted.

Larger items require a special quilting frame which consists of two long bars of wood with webbing or wide tape, tacked on to the inner edge to hold the material, the rollers, and two shorter pieces, the stretchers.

The rollers are pegged into position on the stretchers (figure 56). It helps to have a stand or trestle for the frame, otherwise it must rest between the backs of two chairs. A

full size quilt requires rollers at least 229 cm (90 in) long.

Templates

These are cut from stout card, and can be built up from simple shapes such as a leaf, flower or cup.

Fabrics

Top or outer layer fabric should be of good quality, closely woven, soft with a smooth surface, washable and colour fast. Cottons, Dupion, pure silk, shangtung, fine wool, nun's veiling and fine linen are all suitable. Shiny fabrics should be avoided as they detract from the design. The interlining can be the traditional filling of well washed sheep's wool, which is light, warm and easy to wash. An old blanket is an economical filling and should be pre-shrunk before use. Domette, a wool interlining and cotton or synthetic wadding, all bought by the metre/yard are ideal for garments.

English traditional or wadded quilting

To the casual observer, traditional wadded quilting may seem subdued beside the free designs used in present-day work.

Seldom were more than two colours, generally pastel shades, used. Worked throughout in running stitch, interest lay in the overall design and two pieces of work were rarely alike. It is interesting to study the various combinations of one or more patterns (figures 54, 55).

Methods of working

Having decided the article you wish to make, it is vital to keep the scale of the design in proportion with the size of the object. It is helpful to draw up a plan before marking out the pattern on the fabric. A design for a cushion cover needs to have the emphasis on the centre, whereas a bed quilt requires the centre design to fit the shape of the bed. It should be borne in mind that the stitching holds the three layers of material

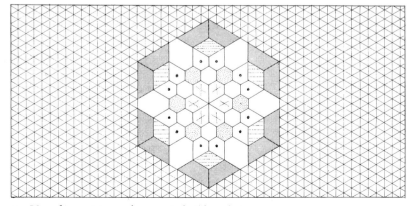

53 Use of isometric graph paper to build up design

together, and prevents puckering. The maximum unquilted area that can be left unworked is 5 cm (2 in) wide in either direction.

Marking the patterns

When the pattern is decided upon, it is marked out on to the unmounted top fabric. To mark the patterns, lay the top fabric right side up on a flat surface, covered with a thick towel or blanket. With the yarn needle mark round the templates, pressing firmly to give a clear impression on the fabric. The area between the design is filled in with parallel straight or diagonal lines, using a ruler.

Setting up work in the frame

Tack either end of the backing to the roller webbing (figure 56). Roll the material round the far roller so that about 45 cm (18 in) is left exposed. The stretchers are then secured in place between the rollers. The work should be firm but not tight. Lay the interlining on to the backing and allow it to hang over the far roller. If wool is used, this must be laid on evenly and each time the work is wound on to the front roller, more wool is added. The top fabric, with the pattern marked on it, is then laid to fit over the interlining and backing. All three layers are firmly tacked together along the front. The weight of the interlining and the top fabric hanging over the far roller helps to keep the work taut. On either side, pin the tapes at about 7.5 cm (3 in) intervals. Temporarily fasten the fabric on the far side with fine pins, or with needles used as pins, keeping them along the line of the pattern to avoid marking the fabric.

Stitching

With the frame set at a convenient height, the design is worked in small even-running stitches which must go through all three layers of material. The needle should be inserted, as upright as possible, from the front to the back of the work,

54 *Traditional quilting patterns— goose wing*

then returned to the front, keeping one hand behind the work. At least two or three stitches are worked before drawing the thread through. The stitching is worked from the bottom right-hand side of the frame. Stitch up and across, to keep the work smooth. To ensure continuity in the pattern, especially in the straight filling lines, it is an advantage to carry on different parts of the design using a number of threaded needles. Each needle is taken a short distance, to keep the line moving evenly across the work. The thread is anchored by running it through the interlining, a little

way from the starting point, coming out and working a back stitch to secure the thread. To finish off a thread, take it through the interlining for some way, back stitch, and lose the end in the interlining.

When the pattern on the unrolled portion is completed, this part must be rolled up to bring forward further material to be quilted. First remove the tape from the sides, by unfastening the pins. The pegs are then taken out to enable the stretchers to be removed. Wind the quilted area of the work on to the near roller, while the appropriate amount is unwound from the other. When

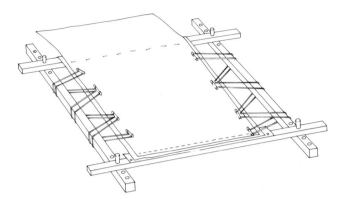

56 *Quilting frame set up with top fabric hanging over top roller*

this is done, the stretchers and pegs are replaced. Prepare the next area to be worked by needling and taping the unquilted material.

When only a small area of quilting is required, the top surface is tacked on to the interlining and attached securely to a larger sheet of backing material that is secured to the frame in the normal manner.

Making up the work

When the quilting is complete, remove the work from the frame and finish off by one of the following three methods.

The quilting method The edges of the top fabric and backing are turned in 1·25 cm ($\frac{1}{2}$ in) and a row of running stitches worked as near to the edge as possible (figure 57). Make sure that the interlining goes to the edge. Work a second row of stitches 1·25 cm ($\frac{1}{2}$ in) inside the first row. The stitching should be equal to those worked throughout.

The piping cord method The edges are turned in and a covered piping cord inserted between (figure 58). Care should be taken to ease the piping cord round corners so that the quilting is not puckered. This finish is advisable for anything that is subjected to wear, as it acts as a protection to the quilting and can be replaced when it is worn.

The binding method The edges of the work are bound with a bias strip of material, which is turned in and hemmed over the raw edges (figure 59). This method is often seen on American quilts.

When quilted material is required for garments, it is removed from the frame, the pieces cut out with a seam allowance and made up with the usual dressmaking processes, but it is advisable to join the seams by hand for greater accuracy.

Bolster cushion

61 cm (24 in) long 20 cm (8 in) diameter

Materials required

0·7 m ($\frac{3}{4}$ yd) plain fabric for top

0·7 m ($\frac{3}{4}$ yd) fine cotton or muslin for backing

0·7 m ($\frac{3}{4}$ yd) cotton or synthetic wadding for interlining

1·5 m (2 yd) piping cord, pre-shrunk

Pad to fit, or equal volume of synthetic stuffing

Cotton or silk thread to match top fabric

Templates for design

Yarn needle

Sewing equipment

Method

The bolster tube and its two ends are marked out and worked on one piece of material, which is only cut up when the quilting is complete. The chosen design is marked out using the templates, ruler and yarn needles. A suggested design is shown in figure 60. Mount the work on to the quilting frame, taking care to keep all three layers smooth. Stitch the design with neat even-running stitches, remembering that the back of the work should look as even as the front. When the quilting is complete, remove it from the frame. Cut the worked areas out, allowing 1·25 cm ($\frac{1}{2}$ in) for turnings. Make up the tube with the right side of the work on the inside. Turn right side out and apply piping cord to both

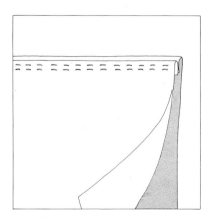

57 *Edges joined with two rows of running stitch*

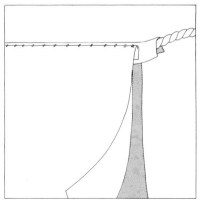

58 *Edges joined by insertion of piping cord*

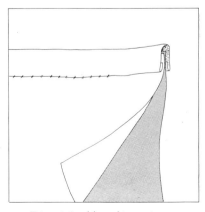

59 *Edges joined by a bias strip*

ends. Finally add one of the worked ends, insert the pad or synthetic stuffing, then attach the other end.

Machine quilting

Using the sewing machine, it is possible to produce a piece of quilting very quickly, with uniform stitch. It is very suitable for making fashion garments and other small items. Although it is not necessary to mount the work in a frame, it is not as simple as it may appear. Manoeuvring a large bulky item under the arm of a sewing machine, while keeping the quilting even and smooth, can be very difficult.

If you plan to quilt by machine, you must baste or tack your work quite closely. Make sure that your interlining is not too thick. A sheet of cotton flannel is possibly easier to manage than cotton or synthetic wadding, which should be no more than 5 mm ($\frac{1}{4}$ in) thick.

Adjust the stitch tension according to the thickness of the work before sewing, about eight stitches per 2·5 cm/1 in. Sew in straight lines, horizontally, vertically or diagonally, from one edge to the other. Stitch the centre rows of quilting first. Check each line of stitching as you complete it, to make sure that there are no puckers on the back.

Decorative stitching The swing needle machine permits the use of a decorative stitch for quilting, which will vary with the type of machine.

Twin needle stitching By using a twin needle you can produce two parallel, closely spaced decorative lines of stitching simultaneously. A straight or zigzag stitch can be used and each thread can be a different colour on the top surface. Only one thread is used in the bobbin, therefore less thread is used.

Machine quilting can be used for decoration or for the more practical purpose of making a garment which is warm to wear. The following project is in the latter category and can be made cheaply, using remnants of fabric from the sales counter.

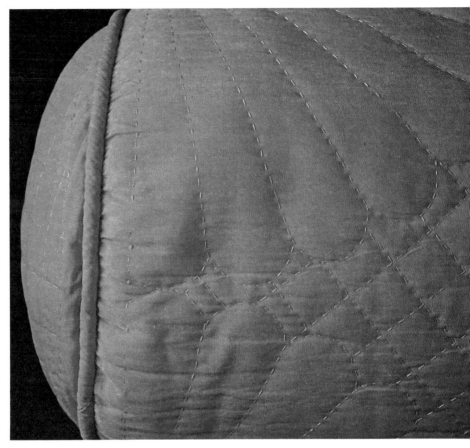

Elegant fan-shaped quilting, worked by hand, adds a touch of elegance to a delicate pink bolster cushion.

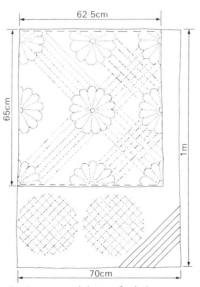

60 Layout and design for bolster cushion

Padded jerkin
Materials required
1·25 m (1·5 yd) of closely woven, patterned cotton fabric for top surface

1·5 m (1·75 yd) of fine matching cotton for the lining and bias strip

1·25 m (1·5 yd) cotton or synthetic wadding for the interlining

Matching sewing thread

Dressmaker's squared paper for cutting pattern

Ruler and pencil

Sewing equipment

Method
Prepare the paper pattern by enlarging the pattern for the front and back sections on to the dressmaker's squared paper (figure 61). Complete the back half of the pattern. The front pattern of the jerkin is reversed when marking out the second front. Cut out the patterns and tack round them on the top surface of the

This jerkin was made from fabric quilted before being cut to shape.

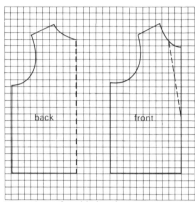

61 *Plan of padded jerkin pattern— square = 2.5 cm (1 in)*

fabric. Do not cut until quilting has been worked. Allow a space between each pattern piece, as sometimes the material creeps into the stitching. Place the lining material face down on a flat surface. Cover with the interlining material, then the top fabric, right side up. Pin, then neatly tack all the materials together at regular intervals over the area.

To quilt, use a twin needle in the machine. Work rows of straight stitches vertically up and down the shapes. Start from the centre of the back and work out to the armholes in each direction. The rows of stitching should be approximately at 5 cm (2 in) intervals apart. Fasten thread ends securely. The two front portions are stitched in the same way, making certain the position of the rows match those on the back at the shoulder seams.

For the final make up, check the pattern on the work, cut out the back and two fronts. Stitch the shoulder and side seams only of the top fabric allowing 1·25 cm ($\frac{1}{2}$ in) for seams. Press seams open. Trim interlining to fit and tack lightly to top seams. Trim and turn in lining material to fit. Slip stitch pieces together.

To bind the edge of the jerkin, prepare strips of bias from the lining material or other contrasting fabric, measuring 3·5 cm (1$\frac{1}{4}$ in) wide. Join the strips together to form a strip 1·7 m (67 in) to bind the edge of the jerkin, and two strips 70 cm (27$\frac{1}{2}$ in) long for binding the armholes. Stitch the strips to the edges of the jerkin, right sides together, 6 mm ($\frac{1}{4}$ in) from the edge. Turn binding to the inside of the jerkin, turn in the edges 6 mm ($\frac{1}{4}$ in), then slip stitch to the lining.

Other forms of quilting

Italian quilting Purely decorative, it is worked by hand or machine, using two layers of fabric. The design is outlined by two rows of parallel stitching, each about 6 mm ($\frac{1}{4}$ in) apart. Quilting wool or thick yarn is then threaded through the channels, on the reversed side, to give a raised effect. This method is commonly used for cushion covers.

Shadow quilting Worked with two layers of material, the top is a transparent fabric, such as georgette. A delicate effect is achieved by threading through coloured wools.

Trapunto quilting Used for padding out large areas of a design, it gives a raised effect and is a suitable technique for working a design on a skirt or jacket. Normally, two layers of fabric are used and the muslin backing is slit. Cotton or synthetic filling is inserted into the back of the work and the slit caught together again.

Linen quilting Worked on linen with a linen scrim backing, it is nearly always carried out in monotone. It is solely for decoration and not for warmth. The stitchery should be in back stitch with a silk thread. A fine cord or wool is threaded through from the back, to areas which require high relief.

Corded quilting Back stitch, on one thickness of material only, across a piping cord held against the work on the reverse side.

Suppliers of templates, threads and quilting accessories

patchwork templates	J. E. M. Patchwork Ltd (manufacturers), Forge House, 18 St Helen's Street, Cockermouth, Cumbria available from local craft shops
traditional quilting frame	details available from The Quilt Circle Secretary, Caroline Fielding, Flat 8, 20 Queens Road, Tunbridge Wells, Kent
traditional quilting patterns	obtainable from The Council for Small Industries in Rural Areas, 35 Camp Road, Wimbledon Common, London SW19
threads	Gütermann available from local shops
silk threads	Gütermann available from local shops The Silver Thimble, 33 Gay Street, Bath Avon BA1 2NT

From geometry to fantasy

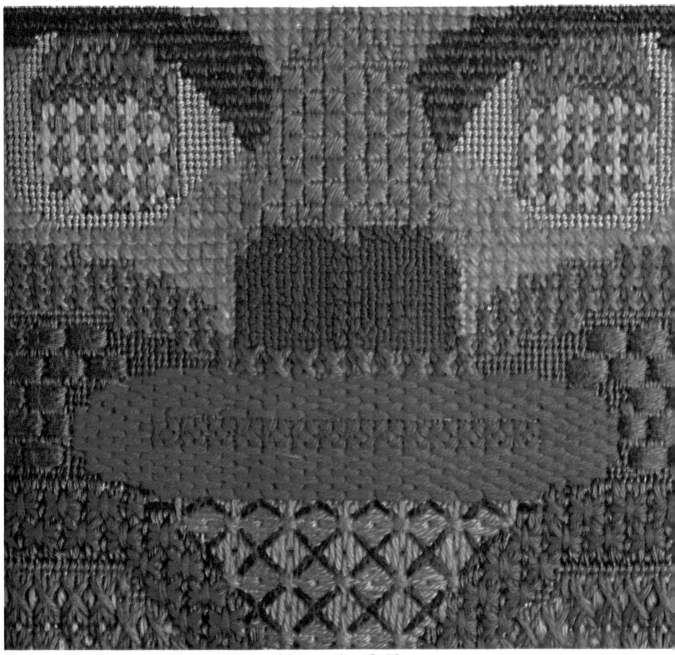

Canvas work can be adapted to a very wide range of designs and motifs. The patterns can be geometric or impressionistic, conventional or with a touch of fantasy. It is a centuries old form of embroidery. All the materials needed are readily available. Tastefully and skilfully used, canvas work can add distinction and a thoroughly personal touch to any home. The basic techniques and stitches are explained and many ideas are illustrated.

The soothing craft

Canvas work is a soothing and satisfying craft. Soothing because of the repetitive nature of the stitches, which can be rhythmical without becoming boring. Satisfying because each stitch is exact, calculated to go over a certain number of threads in a certain direction and can instantly be seen to be correct. There can be no doubt, as in free embroidery, about whether it should be slightly longer or shorter or sloping slightly this way or that. The interest in modern canvas work lies in the variety of stitches used, the range of colours and textures of yarn available, and in designing the particular article you wish to make.

What articles are suitable for canvas work? Chair seats, stools, cushions and kneelers are among the most popular, but the range is very wide. Articles of clothing such as belts, slippers, caps and waistcoats. Accessories such as brooches, pendants, watch straps, all types of handbags, holdalls, spectacle cases, furnishing items such as workboxes, pelmets, firescreens, panels, bell pulls, wastepaper baskets, lampshade bases, rugs, door stops, finger plates and personal items such as book covers, pincushions, needlecases, pencil cases, writing cases and blotters take on fresh and exciting aspects when done in canvas work.

They can be as small and dainty as a bride's headband or as large and solid as a bedhead, as functional as a napkin ring or as decorative as a wall panel.

Whatever object you plan to make you will have to decide the size and shape of the finished piece of work, before you start to embroider. The point about canvas work is that you are creating a new fabric out of canvas and yarns and you will want to embroider the actual shape and size not, as in weaving, to create the fabric and then cut it to size. For a small and dainty piece of work you will need a fine canvas with fine threads or a coarse canvas with thick threads for

This example of a pincushion is made on 13s canvas and is a variation on the smaller one shown in this book with the inclusion of two sets of four Berlin star corner motifs.

something as heavy and hard wearing as a rug.

Different canvases

In the UK, canvas has traditionally been woven with a certain number of threads to the inch and referred to by this number: 12 threads to the inch is called 12s; 16 threads to the inch, 16s.

The varieties of canvas can be soft or stiff, woven with single threads (figure 1) or with double threads to the inch (figure 2).

Soft canvas is preferred by some experienced workers, but it is not easy to buy and is not recommended for beginners. Stiff canvas in a double weave is often sold in packs with a design already painted on and in some cases already trammed. Tramming means laying a yarn along a row of canvas threads and working a sloping satin stitch over it. This stitch is called gobelin: or a straight satin stitch, called straight gobelin (figure 3).

Double canvas can also be used for Florentine work and for stitches with an even number of threads, but these stitches can also be used on single canvas, as well as a number of other stitches. All the objects mentioned here are made in single

canvas threads still showing, or the stitches can be gone over again to make them thicker. Of course, this doubles the amount of work.

Many other yarns can be used to give a variety of colour and texture, as in the white bag and spectacle case, raffene and knitting mixtures with lurex threads used in small quantities can give highlights to a piece of work that threatens to become dull. Knitting wools, nylons

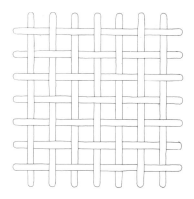

1 Single canvas

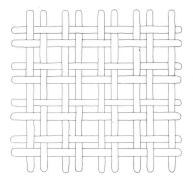

2 Double canvas

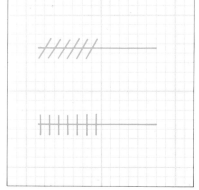

3 Gobelin stitch

canvas in varying grades of thread per inch, from 10s (the coarsest) to 32s (the finest—for a spectacle case).

Yarns

Yarns used for canvas work can vary tremendously but they must relate to the size of the canvas. They must cover the canvas entirely, yet they must also be able to go into the holes usually four times without pulling the canvas too much out of shape. The easiest yarn for beginners to use is Appleton's crewel wool. This is so fine that you can work with more than one yarn, adding as many yarns as required for a particular canvas. This yarn is produced in a wide range of colours.

Appleton, Penelope and Coates

(Tapisserie) produce tapestry wools in a good range of colours. They are mothproofed and easy to use. But the embroiderer is limited in the size of canvas that can be used, usually 18s single or 10s double, and certain stitches need either finer or thicker yarns to be successful. It is always worthwhile to experiment with short lengths of yarn and a variety of stitches before embarking on a large piece of work. It is just as disastrous to have a piece of canvas badly pulled out of shape by using yarns that are too thick, as it is to use yarns that are too fine and produce a canvas insufficiently covered. In the latter event you can sometimes do back stitches between the rows of stitches to cover up any

and mixtures can give unusual effects. Sylko perlé, cotton perlé and stranded embroidery cottons and silks can be used to good effect but you must always select yarns bearing in mind the wear and tear the finished object will undergo. A decorative panel can give full scope to any number of yarns, but a chair seat will have a lot of wear and so harder wearing wools should be selected.

Needles

Needles used for canvas work are called tapestry needles and come in many sizes. Sizes 26–22 are useful for the finer yarns and canvas; 20–18 cover the middle range, and 16–13 are used for the heavier thrums and rug wools. These needles have wide eyes which take the wools and other yarns easily, like crewel and darning needles, but unlike these they have blunt points. This is to ensure that they can go easily through the holes of the canvas, pushing aside any other yarn which is already in the hole, without piercing or splitting it, so that a finished piece of work will have all the working threads undamaged, lying side by side to give a good even tension.

Working on a frame

In canvas work, in order to get good results, it is better to work in a frame. This should be supported against a table or between two tables, chair backs, trestles, or on a special stand so that the worker can sit facing it and have both hands free.

Use yarns not more than 35 cm (14 in) long. A longer yarn can easily wear thin by constantly being pulled against the canvas threads. This spoils the finished work by making it uneven. A fresh yarn should not be made obvious by being thicker than the old one. Even if you have to stop and start more frequently, it is well worthwhile.

Start with a knot, putting your needle in from front to back to allow the knot to rest on the top of the work. The yarn will go along the back of the work to be covered

by the first row of stitches (after which the knot can be cut off). Take the needle at the back of the work with your other hand and put it through from back to front with the same hand to be received by the hand on top of the frame.

In this way, you are working with one hand on top and one hand underneath the frame. This may at first seem tedious, but with a little patience and practice the work rhythm soon becomes satisfying. This method also produces a more even tension and does not pull the canvas out of shape.

When you come to the end of a yarn, darn it into the back of the work or bring it up to a place at the front which will eventually be

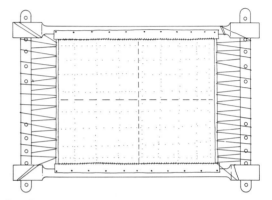

4 Square or slate frame

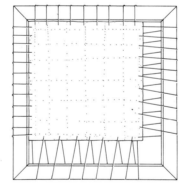

5 Home-made frame with canvas stretched inside

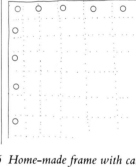

6 Home-made frame with canvas attached by thumb tacks

7 Tent stitch or Petit Point worked in rows

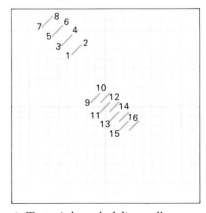

8 Tent stitch worked diagonally

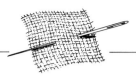

covered at the back. Unlike other pieces of embroidery, canvas work does not require a tidy back since it is always made up into some object and the back of the work is covered. Some teachers even advise leaving all the ends of wool at the back to make extra padding to a finished piece of work. It is undoubtedly true that the more padding a canvas has from the yarns used for the embroidery, the better wear it will give.

A square or slate frame can be bought at most craft shops. This consists of two stout pieces of wood with webbing attached and two side pieces called stretchers, with holes and pegs to fit. Mark the webbing at the centre point.

To frame up a piece of canvas, which should not be wider than the length of webbing on the frame, bind the side edges with strips of fabric. Alternatively, masking tape can be stuck over the edges, or each edge can be turned over 2·5 cm (1 in) and machined down twice, once at the fold and once at the hem turning. Overcast the top and bottom of the canvas either by hand or with a zigzag machine stitch. This prevents it from fraying. Turn 2·5 cm (1 in) of hem, mark the centre and align this with the centre mark on the webbing, wrong sides together.

Overcast firmly, working from the centre points towards the sides to make sure the canvas is in the centre of the frame when finished. If the canvas is longer than the stretchers, roll the excess round the top and bottom bars so that when the stretchers are put in and the pegs are fixed, each end of the canvas is as tight as a drum. Finally, lace the sides over the stretchers with string, leaving about 5 cm (2 in) between each point (figure 4). For very small pieces of canvas, an old picture frame, or four pieces of wood made into a square, can be used. The canvas can then be put into the space and laced to the outside (figure 5), or thumb tacked to the wood (figure

6). In each case make sure that the canvas edges are firmly overcast or bound to prevent fraying.

In all canvas work the stitches are designed to go over set numbers of threads, either vertically, horizontally or diagonally. You should always remember to count threads, not holes.

When the canvas work is completed, it should be stretched before it is made up. To do this, put it on a board which has already been covered with a piece of white fabric.

Begin by fixing one straight edge to the edge of the board with thumb tacks or tin tacks not more than 1 cm ($\frac{1}{2}$ in) apart. Then make one of the sides lie at right angles to this and fix this firmly in the same way.

If the canvas has been pulled out of shape during the embroidery, you may have to dampen it at this stage to pull it into a true rectangle. But in any case, you must wet it again when you have put the tacks in all the way round. Leave it to dry out in a warm room or airing cupboard. Never press canvas with an iron since this spoils the appearance of the stitches and does more harm than good.

Designing for canvas work can be done in various ways. For geometrical designs you can allow the stitches themselves to fall into patterns, straight lines, squares, rectangles or triangles, as for the handbag and pincushion designs.

The problem of having a design with curved lines is easily overcome. Place a drawing of the correct size you require under the canvas. Make sure the lines of the drawing are thick enough to show through the open squares of the canvas. Then, taking a fine brush with waterproof ink, or a laundry marker, draw the design directly on to the canvas. Do not use any type of paint or ballpoint ink which might run when you are dampening and stretching the finished work. When working this type of design, start in the middle of each area with whatever stitch you

require, going up to but not beyond the drawn line. Fill in any irregular edges with tent stitch or petit point. This stitch covers one crossing thread of canvas sloping from bottom left to top right (figures 7, 8). In each case the needle comes up at 1, down at 2, up at 3, down at 4 and so on.

Tent stitch is the most common and useful stitch in canvas work, and can be used to cover large background areas. When large areas are to be covered in tent stitch it is important to maintain an even tension. The best results will be obtained if you work diagonally. If you find this difficult, or the area is not suitably shaped, work in rows, always ensuring that the stitches on the back of the work are sloping, not straight, and longer than those on the front.

Designs can also be worked out on graph paper, and for those who are used to following a chart, this may be the most satisfactory way. But for beginners it may be confusing as each square on a chart represents a thread on the canvas.

Kneeler in Florentine stitch

Florentine is a popular form of canvas work. The stitches are worked vertically, covering the fabric fairly quickly, and can have many variations in the length and the zigzag arrangements of the stitches and also in the colour arrangements. Florentine is only a satin stitch worked in a zigzag fashion over a set number of threads, and once you have set in the first row accurately, every other row is a copy.

To make the kneeler in Florentine stitch (figure 16), take a piece of canvas at least 52 x 37 cm (21 x 15 in).

Frame up and run tacking thread to mark the centre both ways. The kneeler is worked in crewel wool:
Blue 50 g (2 oz) no 929 (darkest)
      25 g (1 oz) no 926
      25 g (1 oz) no 924
      25 g (1 oz) no 922

green 25 g (1 oz) no 337 (darkest)
25 g (1 oz) no 335
25 g (1 oz) no 333
50 g (2 oz) no 331

Using four threads of darkest blue (929), work the Berlin star (figure 10) 15 cm (6 in) towards the top from the centre point each side of the tacking line. The 15 cm (6 in) mark is outside the Berlin star (figure 9).

Work 34 Berlin stars on each of the long sides and 20 on each of the short sides, keeping within the 37 x 22 cm (15 x 9 in) (figure 11). When this outline of Berlin stars is complete, go back to the centre point of the kneeler, and using four strands of blue wool (929) follow the diagram, always working over six threads (figure 16).

Repeat pattern, this time in the second palest shade of green (333) and continue the sequence right across the centre of the kneeler. When this line is complete, go back to the central blue panel and work above the darkest blue with the next shade (926), then 924 and then the palest (922). These will all be over six threads. The next group are only over two threads, but step up or down in exactly the same way as you have already done and use the same blues in the same sequence. You will find the top and bottom of the panels have to be adjusted to stop at the line of Berlin stars. That is why it is best to start every panel in the centre.

When the top of the kneeler is

completed, the sides are worked in rice stitch, or crossed corners (figure 17). The large crosses over four threads are worked in the palest green (331) and the corners are crossed with the darkest blue (929).

Work six rows of this stitch on each side of the kneeler beyond the outline of Berlin stars, leaving the corner squares (figure 12).

When all the work is completed, take it out of the frame and stretch. When completely dry, join the corners up, folding them so that right sides are together (figure 13). Starting at the outside, work backwards and forwards with stab stitches and a strong linen thread until it is quite firm and no canvas shows on the right side. Cut away to leave 1 cm ($\frac{1}{2}$ in) and snip up into the corner so that it will open out.

When all the corners have been stitched, put in a piece of bonded foam of the correct size 37 x 22 cm (15 x 9 in), half as deep again as the sides, 25 cm (3 in) deep for a 5 cm (2 in) deep kneeler. Then add a piece of hardboard 37 x 22 cm (15 x 9 in) which has had the corners sandpapered so that they are smooth and rounded. Take some strong string, linen thread or nylon and starting in the centre lace from top to bottom, tightening as you go so that the foam is being compressed all the time (figure 14).

Do this both ways, although this may seem tedious it is well worth the really firm result. Bonded foam

The Florentine kneeler; detail showing chevron border worked in crewel wool.

is the strongest and firmest and comes usually in a blue and white speckled colour—not in plain colours. After the lacing is complete place a piece of thin foam over the string and finally put on a piece of black leathercloth 2·5 cm (1 in) wider than the kneeler. Turn it in and buttonhole it all round to the edge of the wool work (figure 15).

Cushions

If you want to adapt either of the kneelers to make cushions, do not work the side pieces. Both designs could stay in their original shape and size, or they could be made smaller or larger, or even into a square by re-planning the edge of the Berlin stars. After the finished embroidery has been stretched, measure a piece of suitable fabric the same size for the back of the cushion. Put the right sides together, then tack and sew firmly all round three sides. Back stitching by hand will be more satisfactory than machining since with a machine it will be difficult to machine near enough to the canvas work to hide any unworked canvas. Turn inside out and slip stitch the fourth side after a cushion pad has been inserted. A handmade cord stitched all the way round makes a most attractive finish.

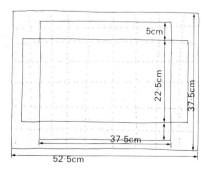

9 Florentine kneeler—marked out canvas

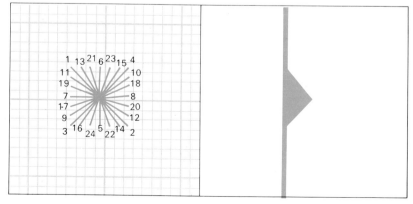

10 Berlin star over 6 threads—outline shows stitch in relief

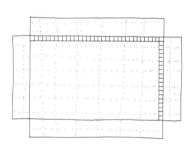

11 Florentine kneeler—Berlin star borders marked on two sides

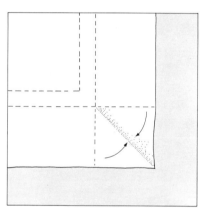

12 Finished worked canvas

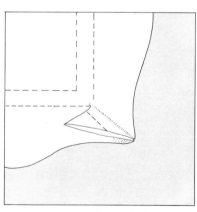

13 Corner of kneeler stitched up

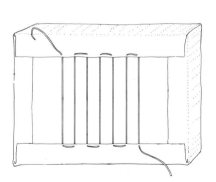

14 Canvas laced in position on hardboard backing

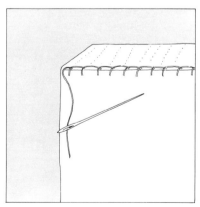

15 Finishing back of kneeler with leather cloth

16 Florentine pattern

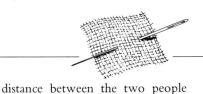

The Florentine kneeler; detail of side panel worked in rice or crossed corners stitch.

Enlarging a design

The Florentine and bird kneelers can very well be adapted to make other objects: cushions, stool tops, chair seats, holdalls or bags. You can also vary the colours and sizes to suit your particular purpose. If you use a coarser canvas and thicker yarns you will get a larger piece of work. Fine canvas and fine yarns produce a much smaller and daintier piece of work.

If you wish to enlarge a design to go on to the same type of canvas, with the same number of threads to the inch, this is the way to do it. Take a tracing of the design and draw a square or rectangle round it (figure 18). Now take a square or rectangle of paper the size you wish the finished design to be and draw the same number of squares or rectangles on it, dividing the area up in exactly the same way, vertically, then horizontally. You will see that the shape in each square or rectangle can easily be drawn into the corresponding larger area to produce a larger version of the original design.

Instructions for making a simple twisted cord

This cord is best made by two people. Yarns are taken from one person to another, each holding a pencil. The end is tied to one pencil and the yarn taken around each pencil in turn. Sufficient numbers of yarns must be stretched round the pencils to equal half the required thickness of the finished cord. The distance between the two people should be approximately two and a half times the length of the cord required.

The end of the yarn is knotted on to one of the pencils. The pencils are then rotated in opposite directions while the yarn is held taut between the two. When the twisted yarn begins to knot into a small loop somewhere along its length, the cord is ready for the next stage.

Bring the two pencils together, and put a third pencil in the middle fold, keeping all very taut. One person now has two pencils and the other person has the third pencil. Twist again, but in the opposite direction. When signs of knotting into a small loop appear, both pull away from each other. This seals the twisting and makes a good firm cord which will not come untwisted or go slack.

Wren kneeler

The design of the kneeler was adapted by Edith John from a piece of fifteenth century glass in the Zouche Chapel at York Minster. It depicts a wren trying to get a fly from a spider's web (figure 19). This forms the centre piece and the design was drawn on to the canvas after centralizing it with tacking threads as described for the Florentine kneeler. The design is framed by Berlin stars in blue, working over six threads of the canvas to form a diamond.

The bird is in red and blue, with heavy cross stitch on its back (figure 20). The wings and tail were worked in multiple rice stitch (crossed corners) (figure 21), and double or Smyrna cross (figure 22) and petit point to fill the spaces.

The tongue and legs were worked in yellow petit point (tent stitch) with back stitches in blue where emphasis is needed. The fly was in red cross stitch (figure 23) with blue back stitches and the web in blue petit point (tent stitch).

The background of the bird design was worked in cream with as many

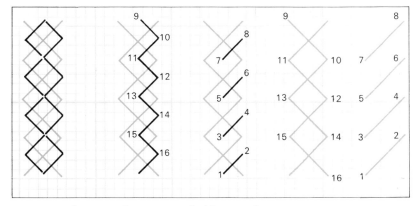

17 Rice stitch or crossed corners, worked in two colours

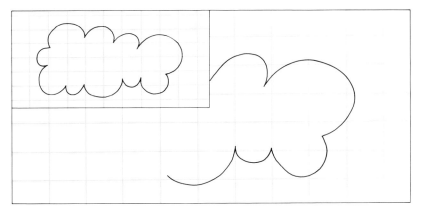

18 Enlarging a design

41

bound crosses as possible over four threads (figure 24), and the rest in petit point (tent stitch).

Two new stitches are needed for the corner areas of the kneeler, both in red; the plaited cross (figure 25) and hound's tooth cross (figure 26).

The outline is again of Berlin stars, with sides of rice stitch (crossed

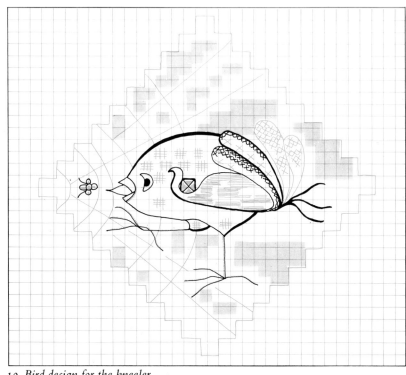

19 Bird design for the kneeler

---

20 *Heavy cross stitch. The second row is worked as for the first, the stitches of the second filling in gaps left by the first.*

21 *Multiple rice stitch, built up in stages upon original cross*

22 *Smyrna or double cross stitch, worked in one and two colours*

23 *Cross stitch*

24 *Bound cross stitch, second stage worked over first three stitches*

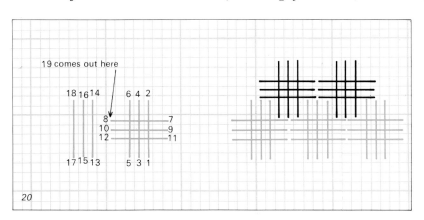

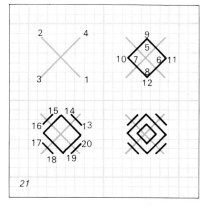

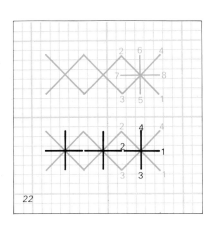

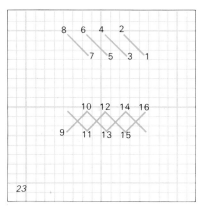

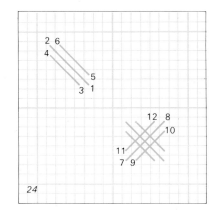

corners) as in the Florentine kneeler. It is made up in exactly the same way. Some churches require a ring to be attached at one end of the kneelers to enable them to be hung up. This is done by folding a piece of strong black tape over a ring (or a D ring which can be bought at DIY shops) and stitching it very firmly to the base of the kneeler before the final leathercloth is sewn on (figure 27).

Brown bag

A 30 cm (12 in) handbag frame with detachable rods
10s canvas 40 x 62 cm (16 x 25 in)
Carpet thrums in browns and yellows

Frame up the canvas and mark the centres both ways with tacking threads. Also mark the approximate finished width of bag 20 cm (8 in) each side of the centre line from top to bottom. Now mark 3·2 cm (1½ in) each side of the centre line going across the canvas. This is for the base of the bag (figure 28).

The base of the bag is worked in long-armed, or long-legged cross stitch (figure 29). This can be done as in figure 30a, working always from left to right, or as in figure 30b, working each row in alternate directions, which gives a slightly different finish.

When the base is completed, each side of the bag is matched. When a row of stitches is worked on one side, it is then repeated on the other.

Working from the base, the first stitch is crossed corners worked in one colour only, with the addition

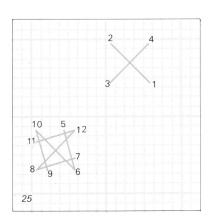

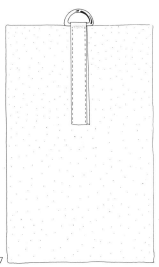

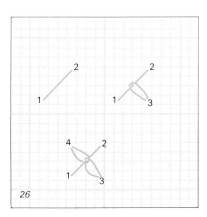

stitch going through loop formed by second stitch and back down again at 4.

25 Plaited cross stitch. Bringing thread out at 5 and in again at 6, follow numbered sequence ensuring that the last stitch from 11 to 12 is threaded under.

26 Hound's tooth cross stitch. Work a diagonal stitch across three crosses of canvas, come up at 3, over and under first stitch and back down at 3, up at 4, over and under original diagonal

27 Attachment of D ring to back of kneeler

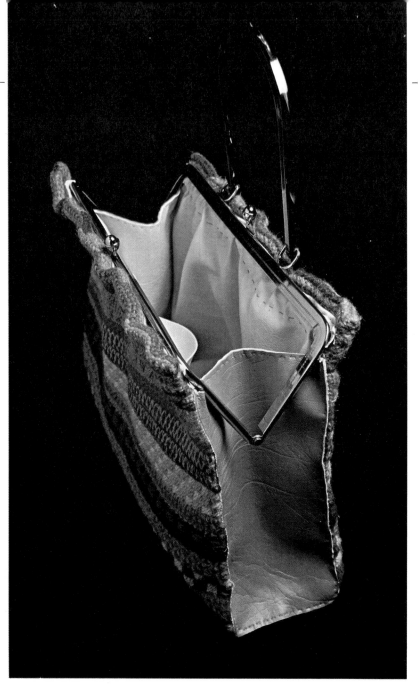

The brown bag worked from thrums in browns and yellows. Side gussets for the brown bag are made from pieces of vinyl anchored firmly to the stitched area, with a pale ivory lining forming an attractive contrast.

of a straight cross on top, remembering to keep the last stitch always going in the same direction, in this case from side to side (figure 31).

The second stitch is bricking, with back stitches top and bottom (figure 32a). The third stitch is flat stitch, worked in two colours, over four threads (figure 32b). The fourth stitch is the same as the first but worked in two colours, and with two rows of it. The fifth stitch is heavy cross (figure 20). The sixth stitch is just a satin stitch over two threads, then hound's tooth cross (figure 26), then another row of satin stitch over two threads, back stitches top and bottom. The seventh stitch is mosaic (three rows) worked over three threads in two allied colours (figure 33). The eighth stitch is oblong cross worked in pale green over six threads (two rows) (figure 34). Straight stitches in dark green cover any exposed canvas threads and back stitches are done top and bottom in dark green. The ninth stitch is long-legged cross stitch worked for two rows from alternate ends (figure 30b). The tenth stitch is Scotch (figure 35) with the tent stitches (figure 7) worked

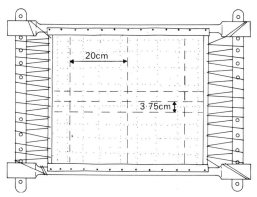

28 Canvas framed up and tacked ready for stitching

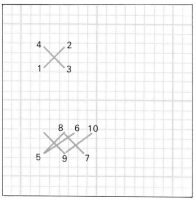

29 Long-legged cross stitch. 1 in first stage becomes 5 in second

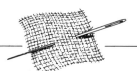

in a slightly different shade of wool.

This completes the main area of the bag except for approximately 6–7·5 cm (2½–3 in) of heading which

Top edge of the brown bag worked upwards in long-legged cross stitch over two rows from alternate ends followed by Scotch stitch with the tent stitches worked in a slightly different shade of wool. (Top right)

Base and bottom edge of the brown bag worked in long-armed (or -legged) cross stitch followed by rows of crossed corners with a straight cross on top, bricking, flat stitch, crossed corners in two colours, heavy cross, satin stitch over two threads, then hound's tooth cross and another row of satin stitch over two threads. These rows are worked upwards towards the top on both sides. (Bottom right)

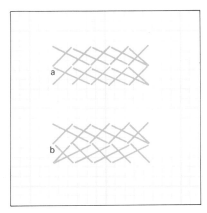

30 *Long-legged cross stitch—(a) left to right, (b) alternate directions*

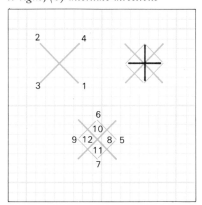

31 *Crossed corners with straight cross on top*

is worked in long-legged stitch (figure 29) but using varying lengths of varying shades of colour.

To make up
Detach the canvas from the frame and stretch. Turn over spare canvas at sides and tack. Fold over the top

32 (a) Bricking stitch over four vertical threads of canvas, (b) flat stitch worked in two colours over four threads, (c) repeated three times to form a square

33 Mosaic stitch. The basic stitch is repeated at each subsequent stage

34 Tied oblong cross over six threads filled in with straight stitches

35 Scotch stitch. One thread is left between each block to be filled in tent.

36 Bag gusset

37 Inserting gussets

and bottom headings so that 1·9 cm ($\frac{3}{4}$ in) of canvas work is on the inside. Tack firmly. Measure a piece of vinyl for the lining exactly to go from side to side and from the canvas work at top and bottom, 35 x 52 cm (14 x 21 in).

If you wish to have an inside pocket, now is the time to position it and sew it in.

For the gussets you will need four pieces of vinyl exactly the same shape, 15 cm (6 in), at the top, tapering to 7·5 cm (3 in) at the bottom and 20 cm (8 in) from top to bottom. Two of these are for the lining and two for the bag itself (figure 36).

Position the centre of the bottom of the gusset for the bag at the centre line of the base of the bag and begin to stitch with stab stitches in a matching strong thread. Make the corner of the gusset match the base of the bag before turning the corner to make the bag side go up the side of the gusset. The top of the gusset

Working upwards, the top section of the white bag is decorated by a row of window eyelet with a tiny pearl in the centre, followed by rows of heavy cross, cross stitch, bricking, double straight cross and finally mosaic stitch. The heading combines alternate rows of gobelin and cross stitch. (Top right)

Base and lower section of the white bag worked in double upright cross for the base followed by a succession of Berlin stars, satin stitch, large cross and straight cross, which involves the subtle use of Twilley's goldfinger for added effect. (Bottom right)

should reach the top of the last Scotch stitch (figure 37).

When the bag gussets have been put in, do the same thing with the lining. Then slip the lining inside the bag and test for size. When you are satisfied with the fit, stab stitch the lining tops to the canvas work which has been turned over. Using

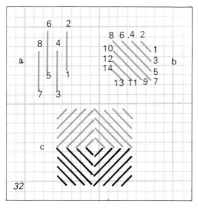
32

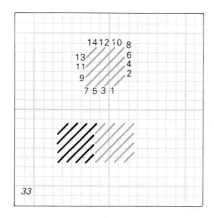
33

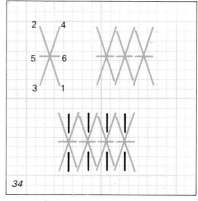
34

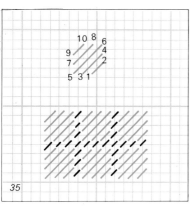
35

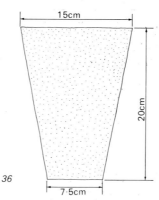
36

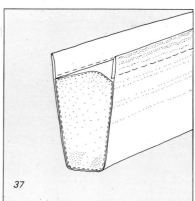
37

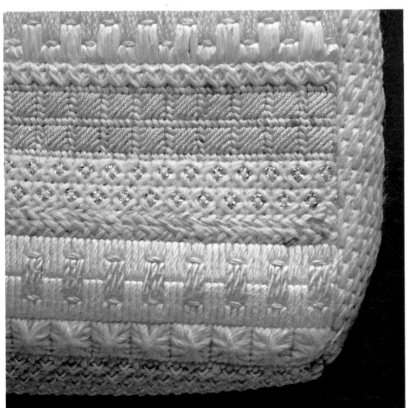

the same stitch work another row about 1 cm (¾ in) below. This makes the slot for the bar of the bag to go through. When this is fixed the hinges fold down outside the gusset, forcing them to fold inside neatly when the bag is closed.

White bag

The white bag is a finer version of the brown one. It is worked on 12s canvas, using a wider range of stitches and yarns and having the gusset worked on canvas.

Here is the list of stitches with the yarns used together with figures of stitches not already described. The base is a double upright cross (figure 38). The straight cross worked in white wool with a white cotton yarn for the smaller diagonal cross.

38 Double upright cross may be worked in two colours using different thicknesses of thread

39 Counted satin stitch

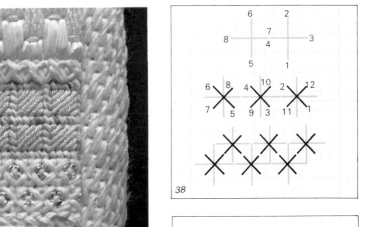

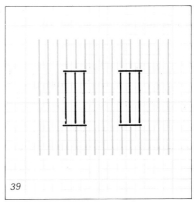

The white bag, worked in a creamy combination of white, ivory and palest gold with an attractive cane handle. The side gussets of the white bag are identical to the brown bag in shape, but in this case worked throughout in bricking.

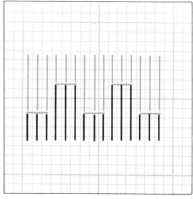

41 Counted satin stitch over six and over three threads

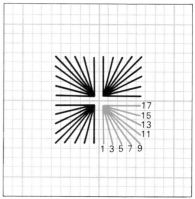

42 Window eyelet stitch with cross of unworked canvas in centre

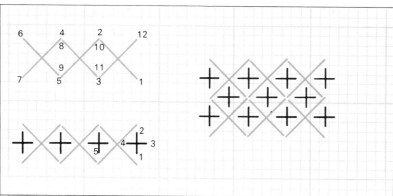

40 Large cross and straight cross. Small crosses fit snugly between the larger ones, with additional crosses between rows.

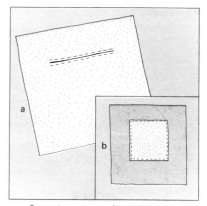

43 Inserting zip pocket—(a) right side, (b) wrong side

No. 1 (from the base) Berlin star over six threads in cream wool. No. 2 counted satin stitch over six and three threads (figure 39). No. 4 large cross and straight cross in white nylon and Twilley's goldfinger (silver) (figure 40). No. 5 Scotch stitch in cream rayon and mottled double knitting wool (figure 35). No. 6 hound's tooth in cream wool (figure 26). No. 7 counted satin over six and three in white raffene and cream nylon (figure 41). No. 8 oblong cross with straight stitches in cream cotton (figure 34). No. 9 window eyelet with a pearl in the centre worked in a white corded yarn (figure 42). No. 10 heavy cross in cream wool (figure 20). No. 11 one row of cross stitch, white nylon (figure 23). No. 12 bricking in white nylon and cream wool (figure 32a). No. 13 double upright cross in cream wool and white cotton (figure

The small pincushion, worked in a subtle blend of blues and greens. Radiating from the centre, the rows are made up of tent stitch, tied oblong cross with back stitch over four threads, a Smyrna cross decorating each corner, straight gobelin over two threads, rice over four threads and the final eight threads remaining on each side in satin stitch. The top is completed by long-legged cross stitch and Smyrna cross.

The side panels of the small pincushion are worked in a combination of blue and green Hungarian stitch.

38). No. 14 mosaic in cream wool and white nylon (figure 33). No. 15 heading, alternate rows of straight gobelin in white nylon (figure 3) and cross stitch in cream wool (figure 23).

The side gussets are worked in bricking (figure 32a) as no. 12 row making them exactly the same shape as in the brown bag. The whole bag is then made up as previously described. If you wish to have a zip pocket instead of an open one, make a slit in the lining and insert the zip putting a pocket at the back of this (figure 43).

Pincushion

The pincushion measures 7·5 cm (3 in) square and requires 24s canvas, approximately 15 cm (6 in) square. It is worked in crewel wool in blues and greens. Beginning at centre, work a square of satin stitch (figure 44). All the other stitches are worked round this square. No. 1 two rows of tent stitch (figure 7). No. 2 tied oblong cross stitch with back stitch over four threads (figure 34) with Smyrna crosses in each corner (figure 22). No. 3 straight gobelin over two threads (figure 3). No. 4 crossed corners (or rice) over four threads (figure 48). No. 5 straight gobelin over two threads (figure 3). No. 6 work the corners (figure 45).

This leaves eight threads each side to be worked in satin stitches in two colours (figure 46a). No. 7 long-legged cross stitch (figure 29). No. 8 Smyrna cross stitch (figure 22).

This completes the top. The sides are worked in Hungarian stitch in two colours for 1·4 cm (½ in) (figure 46b). After stretching, join the corners as in the kneeler, but instead of using a piece of foam for the

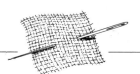

centre stuffing, make an inner cushion from a piece of closely woven fabric such as linen to the exact shape and size of the canvas work and fill with washed sheep's wool or bran. But note that if you are using bran this should be steri-lized by baking before using.

After filling the inner cushion, fit the canvas work over this, pulling the unworked canvas over the bottom and tacking firmly into position. Finish off the bottom with a piece of matching fabric.

45 A square of diagonal stitches

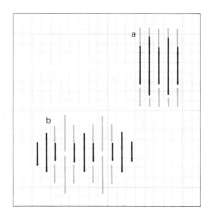

46 (a) Satin stitch over eight threads and (b) Hungarian stitch

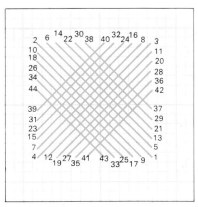

47 Interlacing stitch (large pincushion)

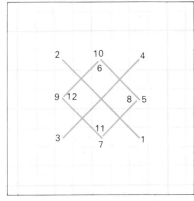

48 Rice or crossed corners stitch, in one colour

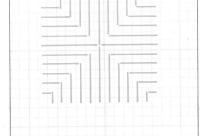

44 A square of satin stitches

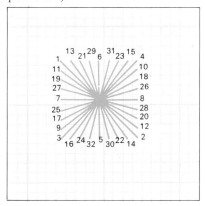

49 Berlin star over eight threads (large pincushion)

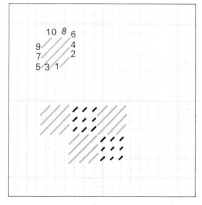

50 Chequer stitch alternating with blocks of tent (large pincushion)

Double needlecase

This double needlecase has a centre pocket for scissors and thimbles. The finished size is 20 x 12 cm (8 x 5 in), so you will need one piece of canvas 30 x 22 cm (12 x 9 in) which can be framed up for working, but which will afterwards be cut into two pieces for making up. Put tacking lines down the centre each way as usual, and again down the centre of each half (figure 53).

Start at the centre of each half with eight Berlin stars over six threads (figure 10) along the extra tacking threads, A-B. Then follow the charts which are similar in design but have some different stitches for each side (figures 51, 52). Plan your own colour scheme with scraps of suitable wool or other yarns. The only new stitch is on side 2 and is leaf diaper (figure 57).

Side 1 (figure 51)
A Berlin star (figure 10)
B Satin
C Tent (figure 7)
D Long-legged cross (figure 29, 30)

A double needlecase with a central pocket for scissors and thimbles. The design for the side panel centres round a line of eight Berlin stars.

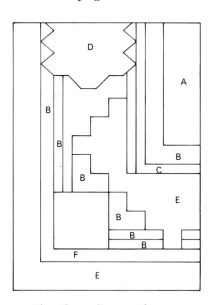

51 Chart for needlecase, side 1

E Heavy cross (figure 20)
F Cross (figure 23)
G Tied oblong cross (figure 34)
H Mosaic (figure 33)

Side 2 (figure 52)
A Berlin star (figure 10)
B Satin
C Long-legged cross (figure 29)
D Leaf diaper (figure 57)
E Crossed corners (figure 48)
F Hound's tooth (figure 26)

To make up
To make the needlecase up you will need a 17 cm (7 in) zip fastener matching your colour scheme, two pieces of lining fabric approximately 55 x 22 cm (21 x 9 in) and two or four pieces of flannel or felt for the needles, 17 x 20 cm (7 x 8 in).

After stretching the finished embroidery, divide the canvas into two pieces and join together again by sewing in the zip fastener. This is easily done by putting the right sides together and sewing firmly with back stitches close to the canvas work stitches. Next, turn all the edges of unworked canvas and the ends of the zip tape to the wrong side and tack firmly.

Turn the raw edges of each piece of the lining on to the wrong side so that they are the correct width to cover the back of the canvas work but are twice the length. Join these pieces together so that the raw edges are on the inside.

Two diamonds of mosaic stitch with inserts of heavy cross stitch in grey surround a row of Berlin stars on the double needlecase.

Now fold the double piece of the lining in half and then each half back on to itself (figures 54, 55).

Stitch C^1, D^1 and C^2, D^2 to the outer edge of each piece of canvas work and the folds X, Y to the zip sides (wrong side of the work). Lastly join A X and B Y to within 6 cm ($\frac{1}{4}$ in) of the zip fastener to form the pocket.

Trim the edges of the pieces of flannel with pinking shears. Fold each in half and stitch along this fold to the stitching line which attaches the lining to the zip.

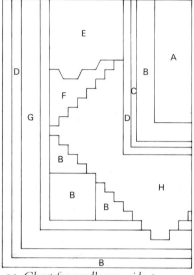

52 Chart for needlecase, side 2

If any unworked canvas shows at the edges where it meets the lining, a handmade cord can cover this, or you can work another row of satin stitch all round, or make a decorative edge with double knot stitch.

You can adapt the needlecase pattern to make a simple needlebook, by avoiding the zip fastener and central pocket. It can be joined together at the centre back, lined with a toning fabric and flannel.

Finishing edge for needlecase
Working from left to right, the yarn is brought up at a corner of the work A. The needle takes a small

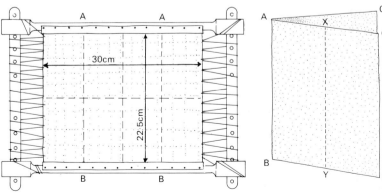

53 Double needlecase canvas framed up

54 Lining for needlecase

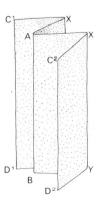

55 Folding lining to form centre pocket of needlecase

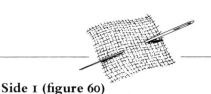

stitch at right angles to the edge line, crossing it and piercing the lining and the canvas work B (figure 56).

Having pulled the thread through, the needle is slipped under the thread from A–B, and then slipped through a second time in the same way but just to the right, and pulled over the working thread to form a button-hole stitch (figure 56).

This stitch varies in appearance according to the distance between A and B. The nearer A and B are together, the closer and firmer this edge stitch will be.

Spectacle case

The spectacle case is worked on very fine canvas, 32s, with appropriately fine yarns. It measures 15 x 9 cm (6 x $3\frac{1}{2}$ in) but the design could be extended if necessary. If you have a case into which your own spectacles fit, place it on a piece of paper and

pencil round the edge to get the size and shape. Remember the depth between back and front and allow for this when you plan your piece of work.

The design was inspired by a totem pole outside a Red Indian exhibition at Expo 67 in Montreal (figures 60, 63).

The two sides are set out full size with stitches, yarns and colours indicated. Most of the stitches have already been illustrated, but details of new ones are given and satin stitch squares and stars are shown in detail. Framing up, centralizing the canvas and marking out the design are all done in the usual manner, as for the bird design. The stitches are started in the middle of each area, working towards the edges and filling in any uneven spaces round the edges with tent stitch in the same colour.

Side 1 (figure 60)

A Satin stitch star in square (figure 61), coton à broder: yellow and red
B Floral cross (figure 62), coton à broder: brick and brown
C Hound's tooth (figure 26), DMC coton perlé No. 12: green
D Multiple rice (figure 21), DMC coton perlé No. 12: blue and magenta
E Smyrna cross (figure 22), coton à broder: peach and brown
F Petit point (figure 7), DMC coton perlé No. 12: pale blue
G Mosaic (figure 33), DMC coton perlé No. 12: darker blue
H Straight gobelin (figure 3), stranded cotton: grey
I Cross stitch (figure 23), DMC coton perlé No. 12: russet
J Multiple rice (figure 21), DMC coton perlé No. 12: pale brown
K Bricking (figure 32a), coton à

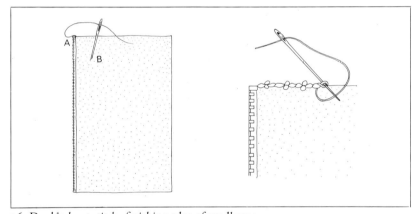

56 Double knot stitch, finishing edge of needlecase

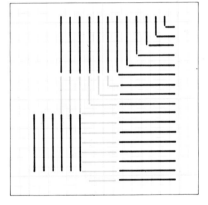

58 Satin stitch squares on side 1

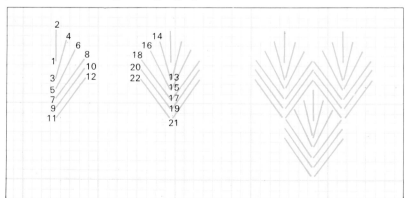

57 Leaf diaper stitch. Working in sequence, the final stitch is brought up from 21 and down through 15 to form vertical stem of leaf.

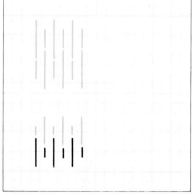

59 Parisian stitch, over a sequence of either 2, 4, 2, 4 or 1, 3, 1, 3 threads

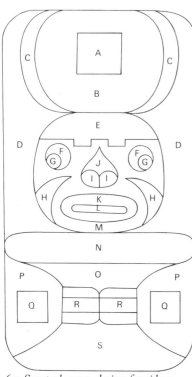

60 Spectacle case, design for side 1

broder: red

L Rice (figure 48), coton à broder: purple

M Cross (figure 23), stranded cotton: peach

N Berlin stars (figure 10), DMC coton perlé No. 12: green

O Bound cross (figure 24), rayon: reddish brown

P Plaited cross (figure 25), coton à broder: pale brown

Q Satin stitch square (figure 58), stranded cotton: magenta and blue

R Petit point (figure 7), DMC coton perlé No. 12: brick and dark brown

S Heavy cross (figure 20), DMC coton perlé No. 12: green

Side 2 (figure 63)

A Berlin stars (figure 10), DMC coton perlé No. 12: green

B Cross (figure 23), coton à broder: brick

C Straight gobelin (figure 3), stranded cotton: dark brown

61 Satin stitch star at top of side 1

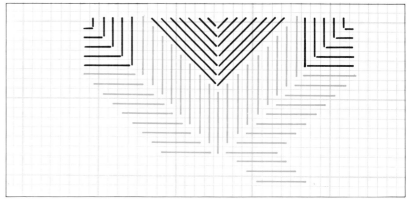

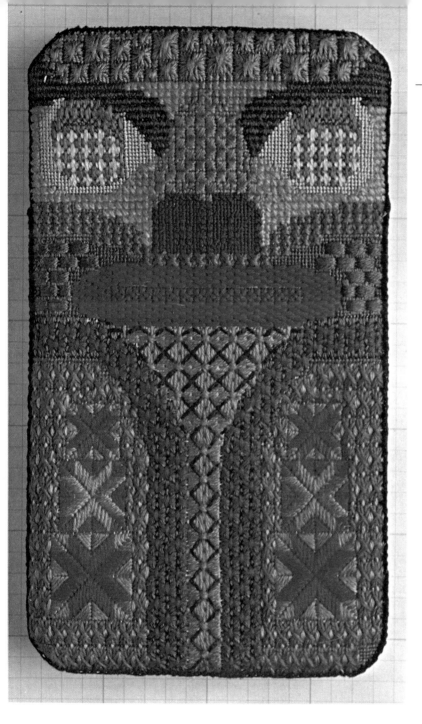

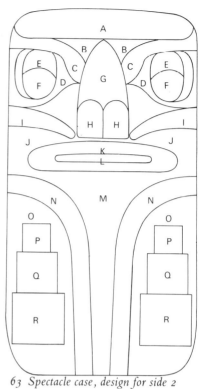

63 Spectacle case, design for side 2

D Petit point (figure 7), DMC coton perlé No. 12: pale blue

E Parisian (figure 59), coton à broder: dark blue

F Mosaic (figure 33), coton à broder: pale and dark blue

G Multiple rice (figure 21), coton à broder: pale brown

H Cross stitch and petit point (figures 23 and 7), DMC coton perlé No. 12: russet

I Hound's tooth (figure 26), coton à broder: pale brown

J Heavy cross and petit point (figures 20 and 7), DMC coton perlé No. 12: green

K Bricking (figure 32a), coton à broder: red

L Rice (figure 48), coton à broder: purple

M Floral cross (figure 62), coton à broder: peach and brown

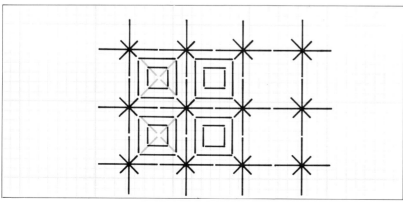

62 Floral cross. Work upright crosses over six threads, crossing at centre. Back stitch round squares in same colour, finishing with stitches radiating from centre of each square in a different colour.

N Raised double cross (figure 64), coton à broder: blue and magenta

O Triple oblong cross (figure 66), coton à broder: tan and yellow

PQR Satin stitch star in squares, three sizes (figure 65), coton à broder: red and peach

To make up

To make up the spectacle case you will need two pieces of stiffening cut to the correct size and shape. A heavy type acetate is ideal as it is light and firm, yet sufficiently pliable to be satisfactory. This can usually be obtained from good stationery shops, otherwise buckram or strawboard could be used. After stretching the canvas work in the usual way, lace the pieces over the stiffening as in the making up of the kneeler. Line each piece separately with soft matching fabric. Velvet is ideal for this as it gives protection to the spectacles from the harsh edges of the canvas. The two

Autumn leaves scattered on a navy background decorate a classic footstool made for the NFWI Chairman's office in London.

sides are joined together with a side gusset, leaving one end and about 5 cm (2 in) of each side free.

There are various ways of making this strip. An easy method is to find a strong petersham ribbon of the right width and colour. You could make a ribbonlike strip from the lining fabric, or work a strip of canvas to the right length and width using some suitable stitch to make it firm yet decorative. Berlin stars, crossed corners, or long-legged cross stitch are only a few of the suitable ones from which to choose. Whatever you decide for the strip, oversewing with a strong matching thread is the best way of fixing it. Finally, a decorative edge of cord or double knot stitch all the way round both sides will make a good finish.

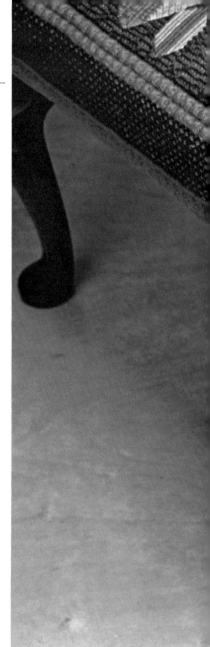

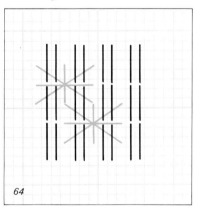

64

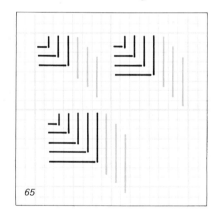

65

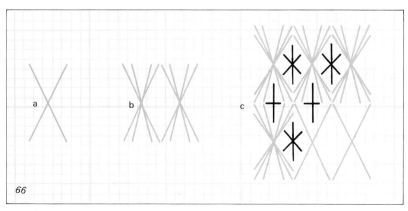

66

64 Raised double cross. Work straight stitches over four threads in groups of two, leaving two threads between each. In a second colour work double crosses over two groups of satin.

65 Satin stitch squares in three sizes

66 Triple oblong cross stitch, (a) work diagonally over 4 × 8 threads, (b) add second cross over 2 × 8 threads, (c) add third cross over 4 × 6 threads. Fill in between crosses in second colour with upright stitch and cross stitch on top. Fill between rows in second colour with an upright cross. Keep final stitch the same (vertical or horizontal).

Footstool

The stool was designed for the NFWI Chairman's room at the London office to match the curtains and chair covers. The pattern used for these had leaves of autumn colours naturalistically placed with very little of the dark navy background showing. The design for the canvas work was made up of two sizes of leaves cut out in paper, strategically placed to form a design (figure 67).

The large leaves have a great many stitches in many shades of browns, russets and yellows. The small leaves are worked in rows of satin stitch

67 Design for footstool

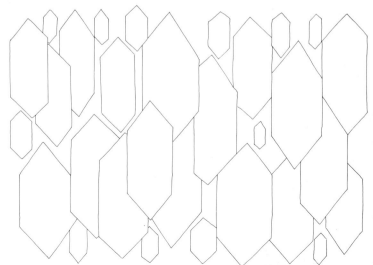

over two threads in tones of one colour. The background is in a very dark navy blue, worked in straight gobelin stitch (figure 3) mostly over three threads but sometimes leaping to five threads, then back to four, two or three, so that no set lines emerge.

In between the rows, back stitches in russet make the gobelin stitches more prominent and cover up any threads of canvas.

Outlines of Berlin star define the top and sides of the stool which was made up in the same way as the kneeler, and fastened to a wooden base with tacks. Finally, a braid made of canvas worked in Berlin stars was stuck all round the base to hide the tacks.

Chair seats

A set of dining room chair seats makes a particularly satisfactory project. The photograph shows one with a very free design planned to complement a very bright vinyl floor covering, which had many colours in it. For each chair one main colour was chosen in four shades for the unusual shapes and a black background for each chair. The shapes emerged by tracing a small area of the floor covering 12 x 10 cm (5 x 4 in) and enlarging it to the size of the seat 47 x 42 cm (19 x 17 in).

Only two basic stitches were used. Berlin stars (figure 10) were worked over varying numbers of threads for the shapes and the areas were shaded from pale to dark quite freely. A large Berlin star over eight threads was worked in the middle of an area. Where there was not sufficient room for this size, a smaller one was worked over six threads, then over four. The edges were filled in with cross stitch over two threads or

A piece of vinyl floor covering inspired this striking seat cover engulfed in orange and red flames.

petit point over one. The background was worked in straight gobelin stitch.

Red holdall

The red holdall was designed to carry folders which are the right size for sheets of drawing paper, or for music. It was made in 10s canvas with a selection of double knitting wools, nylons, fresca, perlita, candlewick cotton and Sylko perlé No. 5. The design was produced from cut pieces of paper such as triangles and rectangles which vaguely represented buildings and roofs. They were moved about on the required shape until they looked satisfactory. Each side is slightly different, although the same shapes were used for each side and the edging pieces also had similar shapes yet gave quite another impression of the buildings. The design was drawn on to the canvas and the stitches started in the middle of each space,

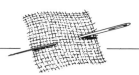

The suggestion of a built-up area in different shades of red covers the side of this good-sized holdall made on 10s canvas.

and stopped when they reached the drawing line for the next space in the design.

The finished holdall measures 40 x 25 x 12 cm (16 x 10 x 5 in) and was stiffened with the heavy type acetate as in the spectacle case. It was lined with blue felt and has a loose bottom inside which can be removed for easy cleaning. The top was supported by a rectangle of lampshade wire made to the exact dimensions, 40 x 12 cm (16 x 5 in) and was held in place by being oversewn with wool. The handles were also of a thick cord made from some of the wools used for the embroidery. (Figures 68, 69.)

Side 1

A Byzantine (figure 70), fresca and perlita: four shades of red

B Double stitch (figure 71), fresca and perlita: golden brown

C Parisian (figure 59), perlita: red

D Smyrna cross (figure 22), double knitting: maroon

E Double upright cross (figure 38), perlita and candlewick: red and pink

F Bound cross (figure 24), nylon knitting: deep pink

G Bricking (figure 32a), fresca: red

H Flat stitch (figure 32b), candlewick and perlita: brick red

I Leaf diaper and tent (figures 57 and 7), knitting mixture Sylko perlé No. 5: brown and brick red

J(a) Hungarian ground (figure 72), knitting wool: red and pink

J(b) Hungarian ground (figure 72), knitting wool: red and pink

K Rice (figure 17), candlewick and stranded cotton: brick red

L Straight upright cross (figure 73), perlita: tan

M Large cross and straight cross (figure 40), candlewick and double knitting: pink and maroon

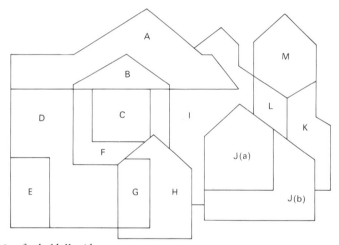

68 Design for holdall, side 1

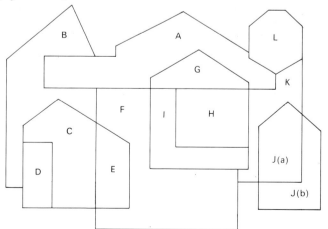

69 Design for holdall, side 2

Side 2

A Byzantine (figure 70), fresca and perlita: four shades of red

B Leaf diaper (figure 57) and tent (figure 7), knitting mixture Sylko perlé No. 5: brown and brick red

C Flat stitch (figure 32b), candlewick and perlita: brick red

D Double upright cross (figure 38), perlita and fresca: maroon and tan

E Bound cross (figure 24), nylon knitting: deep pink

F Smyrna cross (figure 22), double knitting: maroon

G Double stitch (figure 71), fresca and perlita: golden brown

H Parisian (figure 59), perlita: red

I Diagonal Parisian (figure 74), fresca: red

J(a) Hungarian ground (figure 72), knitting wool; red and pink

J(b) Hungarian ground (figure 72), knitting wool: red and pink

K Rice (figure 17), candlewick and stranded cotton: brick red

L Large cross and straight cross (figure 40), candlewick and double knitting: pink and maroon

(Left) A clash of reds and golds continue the geometric theme on the bottom and side panels of the holdall.

(Right) A closer examination of the holdall shows a mass of different stitches worked together in varying shades of red.

70 Byzantine stitch. Stitch length and number worked in each direction can be varied. Each row repeats the first.

71 Double stitch, in one or two colours, showing how subsequent rows are fitted into preceding ones

72 Hungarian ground stitch

73 Straight upright cross, worked in one or two colours

74 Diagonal Parisian stitch

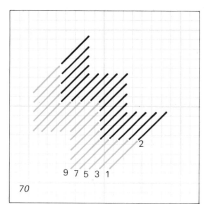

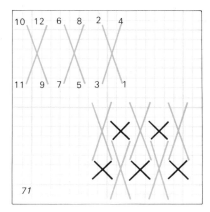

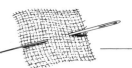

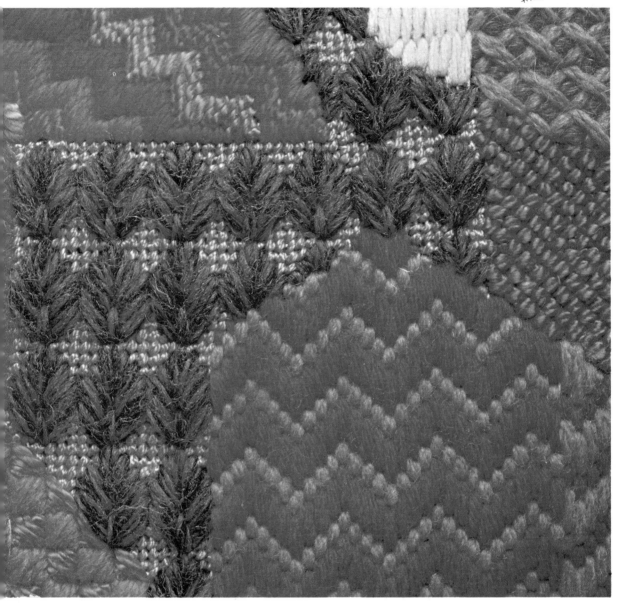

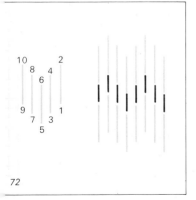

72

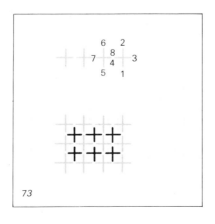

73

74

The patterns previously given for each side of the spectacle case act both as a guide to the areas to be filled by each stitch and to the colours to be used. These can be filled in on the patterns, as this picture shows. This method could be applied to any design you wish to plan in colour.

Suppliers of canvases and Appleton's wools

Mrs Mary Allen,
Wirksworth,
Derbyshire DE4 4BN

Mace & Nairn,
89 Crane Street,
Salisbury,
Wiltshire

Christine Riley,
53 Barclay Street,
Stonehaven,
Kincardineshire AB3 2AR

Teagle Embroideries,
45 Davenport Avenue,
Hessle,
N. Humberside NU13 0RN

Spinning Jenny,
Bradley,
Keighley, Yorks,
BD20 9DD

De Denne Ltd,
159/161 Kenton Road,
Kenton, Harrow,
Middx.

The Handworker's Market,
6 Bull Street,
Holt,
Norfolk

The Royal School of Needlework,
25 Princes Gate,
Kensington SW7 1QE

The Needlewoman Shop,
146 Regent Street,
London W1.

A bridge between the
old and new. . .

In the hands of a skilled operator the sewing machine can produce work every bit as beautiful as traditional hand embroidery. Even a beginner can produce the most effective results. All the basic steps are explained and more sophisticated designs and techniques are included. The craft of machine embroidery forms a perfect example of the bridge that can be achieved between a traditional and time-honoured skill and the modern machine. In this it is probably unique among crafts.

Learning to draw with a needle

The use of the domestic sewing machine for embroidery can open up a whole new world of colour, texture, stitches and creative expression undreamt of by most machine-owners. A considerable capital outlay is locked up in any sewing machine. It therefore makes sense to use your machine to the best possible advantage.

Machine embroidery can vary from simple rows of straight stitching or automatic patterns to the more varied effects of free embroidery. This could be described as drawing with the machine needle, the material being stretched taut in an embroidery hoop or frame and moved by the worker. The use of a swing-needle machine gives the advantage of zigzag and satin stitch; but free embroidery can be worked on most straight-stitch machines provided they are powered by electric motor or treadle, as both hands need to be free. With many modern machines twin needles can be used. These give added interest to automatic patterns, producing tucks and other decorative effects. Thick threads can be couched by machine and the swing-needle is excellent for all appliqué work.

Machine embroidery can be worked on dresses, table linen, soft furnishings and toys, and washes well. It is ideal for embroidered pictures and wall hangings, either alone or used together with beads and hand stitching.

History

The popular demand for embroidery on fashionable dress in the early nineteenth century led to the invention of various embroidery machines. These had many needles which constantly needed rethreading by groups of work girls. At first these early machines could only embroider narrow braids or edgings.

Apart from these commercial multi-needle machines, efforts had

A glimpse of things to come stands on a table surrounded by ladies sewing for a bazaar. (The Girl's Own Paper, London, 1886.)

been made since the end of the eighteenth century to perfect a continuous-thread machine. At first the inventors tried to copy hand chain-stitching, developed from tambour work using a hooked needle. A Frenchman, Barthélemy Thimonnier, patented the first chain-stitch machine in 1830, worked by foot treadle. Since there was no mechanical feed, the worker controlled the flow of the cloth.

The sewing machine as we know it today was the result of a series of inventions, each one an improvement on the last. In 1846 Elias Howe, an American, patented a lock-stitch machine which used two threads, one in the needle and one beneath in the shuttle; but it was not until the middle of the nineteenth century that A. B. Wilson developed the mechanical cloth feed and rotary shuttle. Another American, Isaac Singer, combined all the best ideas and in 1851 his no. 1 machine was patented to become the first prac-

was regarded as art rather than craft. Some extremely fine and beautiful work was produced by the demonstrators in the Singer workrooms on straight-stitch treadle machines, satin stitch being achieved by movement of the embroidery hoop alone. Although industrial trade machines were used in the embroidery workshop from just before the first world war, the girls also worked panels and wall hangings for their own enjoyment on domestic machines.

One of the most talented of the workers was Dorothy Benson, who in 1936 was invited to demonstrate machine embroidery at Bromley College of Art. This revival of free embroidery was partly due to the interest of a new generation of creative embroiderers who sought a fresh and exciting medium to express their interpretation of modern embroidery. Foremost among the students was Rebecca Crompton whose exhibited work caused controversy at the time. It was not until the 1950s, with the help of the Needlework Development Scheme, that machine embroidery became acceptable.

Many improvements were made to sewing machines from the 1920s onwards. Efficient electric motors replaced the treadle, and in 1940 the first domestic free-arm machine was made by Elna. In 1943 Bernina brought out a portable zigzag machine. This in fact revolutionized all domestic machine embroidery, bringing satin stitch and a variety of swing-needle effects into the range of the ordinary machine-user.

The first fully automatic machines with interchangeable pattern cams appeared in the early 1950s. The trend is now for easily dialled or push-button pattern selection. The use of twin needles and reverse-feed action increases the pattern choice even further.

Sewing machines

A sewing machine is a mechanized needle. How it is used depends upon the operator. Like the familiar sew-

tical sewing machine. However, competition from the Wheeler and Wilson company forced him to produce a lighter-weight domestic machine in 1858. This he called the Family machine. In 1865 he brought out the New Family machine, which was assembled in Scotland.

In the 1860s it was possible to work decorative stitches on these lock-stitch machines as the manufacturers supplied special attachments and guides to encourage dressmakers, who found them an invaluable aid to making the richly trimmed fashions of the period.

In 1885 the Singer company introduced the first electric sewing machines, but these did not come into general use until after the first world war.

It was probably around this time that the first embroidery on domestic machines was worked in America. This was free embroidery, worked in an embroidery frame and with the cloth feed mechanism put out of use. Called art embroidery in 1889, the Singer workrooms used this method as an added incentive to popularize the domestic machine. It was never used commercially and

ing needle, it can do both plain sewing and embroidery. If you already possess a sewing machine, this section may help you to find out exactly what kind of embroidery can be worked on your machine. If you are thinking of buying a new machine, it may help you in your choice.

Think twice before parting with an old but reliable machine. The trade-in price is never very high. You could keep your old, solidly built, straight-stitch machine for dressmaking and use a modern machine for embroidery and neatening fabric edges.

If one machine has to be used for both dressmaking and machine embroidery, your choice must be influenced by whichever has the greater priority. If dressmaking is your main concern, then choose as good a machine as you can afford. Like so many other things, you get what you pay for. A good machine can last a lifetime and a reputable firm will give excellent after-service. Never buy a machine in a hurry. Be prepared to see and try out as many different makes as possible. Most firms give demonstrations, but do not be rushed into buying a machine you are not sure about.

A good dressmaking machine should sew quietly with an even top and bottom tension on any fabric. All sewing machines should stop directly your foot is raised from the control and not run on. The bobbin should be easy to fill—one new machine automatically winds the bobbin through the needle. Easy change from straight-stitch to zig-zag and up to twenty automatic embroidery stitches, including stretch stitches, plus an automatic or four-step button-hole, will allow plenty of scope. A free-arm model is a great help for sewing in sleeves and other awkward places.

Most modern machines have a needle that threads from front to back. This means that twin needles can be fitted, and nearly all have a drop-feed device. The latter is often labelled darning. The cloth feed is the tiny row of teeth beneath the needle that controls the flow of cloth, and therefore the stitch length. For free embroidery this needs to be put out of action. Some older models have a cover plate to go over the feed, but this is not entirely satisfactory as the framed material will not lie flat over the raised plate. The additional use of a darning foot can help to overcome this problem.

If your machine is to be used mainly for embroidery, you should bear the following considerations in mind.

Size
Small portable machines do not have enough space beneath the short arm to allow the use of any but the smaller-size embroidery frames. Unless it is to be fixed in position, have as heavy a machine as you can lift easily.

Free arm or flat bed
There is no doubt that a free-arm machine is extremely useful, but even with the addition of the extension table, it is not so firm as the flat bed, especially when used for free embroidery. The ideal embroidery machine is fitted into a workbench or sewing table, so that the worker's arms can rest while moving the frame.

Foot control
This needs to have as great an area as possible in contact with the foot to give maximum control. There is, however, a new foot control that works on air pressure and is very easy to use. Some machines have a variable or slow speed control. Beginners may find this useful, but for all normal work it is not necessary and there can be problems with over-heating, though most motors have a cut-out. The machine is often in continuous use for long periods when working machine embroidery, unlike the intermittent use when dressmaking, and it is a good idea to let it rest from time to time.

Light
All new sewing machines have a built-in light over the needle while older models have a bulb fixed behind. Always sew in a good light.

Top threading
The machine should be easy to thread as you will be constantly changing the colours. In the early machines the thread had to be poked through the holes in the various thread guides. Now most machines have slots or spirals into which the thread slides. In some models you only have to thread the needle, although automatic needle-threaders and open needles can help those who have difficulty. Two separate sets of thread guides prevent threads entangling when twin needles are in use. Numbered top tension is essential. Some machines have a plus or minus sign, but the more divisions, the easier it is to read. See that the thread flows freely through the guides, whatever kind of machine you use.

Needles
Older machines have only one fixed-needle position, but newer machines have three positions: left, right and centre. On simpler semi-automatic machines these needle positions can be used to create patterns and to increase the scope of automatic patterns. Some needles will only fit the machine they are designed for, while others will fit several machines. Check before you use them.

Make quite sure you have the right needle for the job. You can buy special needles for sewing leather, jersey fabrics and synthetics. Some machines have slanting needles. These are not an advantage when working free embroidery with the presser foot removed. It is more difficult to judge where the needle will enter the cloth in relation to the moving embroidery frame. The use of a darning foot will help to ease this problem to a considerable extent, allowing you to see the stitches.

Feet

Most machines come supplied with a variety of feet made for special sewing tasks. This is apart from the normal presser foot for straight or zigzag stitching. Some firms supply a darning foot which allows movement of the material beneath the needle. Thinner fabrics need backing and some embroiderers prefer to use this foot as well as the frame. In the older type of machine, and on cheaper models, the foot is fixed in position with a screw. The machine embroiderer will find it necessary to remove or change the foot frequently. One make of machine has a push and clip-on foot, with a shank

The sewing machine of today. Simple to thread and easily operated with well-displayed controls. Many modern machines offer a wide range of attachments and patterns.

that is both easy to remove or replace, while other machines have a variety of clip-on methods where the foot is removed from the shank. These are all helpful.

Needle plate

This is the removable plate that surrounds the feed dog teeth. Most machines have interchangeable plates, with a single round hole for straight-stitch sewing and a slot for zigzag stitching. In some models it is necessary to unscrew this plate; others have ones that simply lift out or are held with a clip, or are changed automatically. Since it is very important to keep the machine clean and well oiled when working machine embroidery, the easier this plate is to remove, the better.

Presser foot bar lever

This lowers the foot and controls

the top tension. Some machines are now fitted with an additional knee-operated control lever. This leaves both hands free. Even though the presser foot is removed in free embroidery, this lever must be lowered or the machine will not sew properly. New machines have an easily adjustable or self-adjusting pressure knob and some have a variable drop-feed or darning control. This half-dropped position is used when sewing very fine fabrics and it is useful in certain embroidery techniques.

Automatic patterns

Some machines have only a few automatic patterns while others have a large selection which is increased by the use of reverse-feed action and stitch lengthening. One machine keeps the pattern density as well as increasing the length. A large choice of patterns is not necessary, but it can be great fun.

Basically, there are two systems. The first uses pattern cams (or discs) and the second has push-buttons or dials for pattern choice. Sometimes the two systems are combined. The pattern cams are chosen individually and physically slotted into the top of the machine which, when set, sews the required pattern. There is a mark where the pattern begins and ends which is located by a notch. There is a wide choice of patterns and new cams can be added to the set. This method is more bothersome to use, but mechanically there is less to go wrong.

The other type is built into the machines. Colour codes and diagrams help the user to dial the chosen pattern and the machine does the rest. Some machines have an even more sophisticated electronic push-button system. The patterns can be changed in rapid succession and a stop device is built in to limit patterns to one repeat only.

All these machines produce rows of beautiful automatic pattern stitchery. But, to do this, some have sacrificed adaptability, giving the

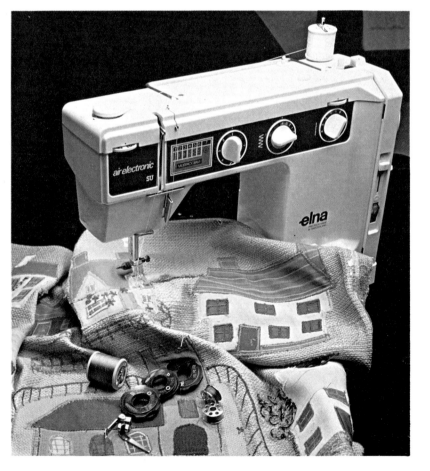

creative embroiderer less control over the machine.

Stitch-width lever or knob

This is very important to the machine embroiderer. Those who are more advanced will want to be able to sew freely in the embroidery frame and at the same time control the stitch-width lever with the right hand. This means that it should be easy to move in a continuous manner.

Some sewing machines have a dialling knob. As long as it rotates freely it is all right, but on some of the fully automatic machines the controls have been simplified to such an extent that it is not possible to do this. Others have a lever in a slot that can be moved sideways. Some can be stiff or work on a ratchet. The ideal method is a lever working on a spring-loaded principle that allows maximum control but also has stops to set the width. One new machine has a knob with extended lever, set low on the machine, and is extremely good. The normal satin-stitch width is 4 mm ($\frac{1}{6}$ in). Two manufacturers produce machines with a throw or width of 7 mm ($\frac{1}{3}$ in). This gives more scope for embroidery and allows extra space for twin and triple needlework. However, fine fabrics need backing when sewing satin stitch as the slot in the needle-plate is correspondingly wider.

Stitch-length lever or knob

A knob, often marked from one to four, is easier to adjust than the vertical screw lever found on older machines.

Bobbin and bobbin case

Your most important choice will be the position of the bobbin case in the machine. All modern machines have round bobbins, in either fixed or removable bobbin cases. If the bobbin case is fixed, it lies horizontally either to the left, behind or in front of the needle plate. A sliding or lifting plate gives access to the

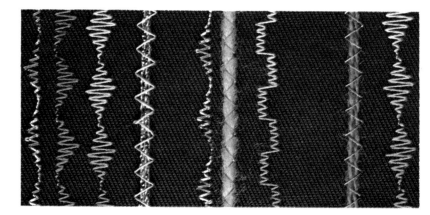

A detail from the patchwork bed-spread shows the versatility of the swing-needle machine by varying the length and width of the stitch. (Top)

An ordinary straight-stitch machine can be used to achieve some remarkably interesting patterns. (Bottom)

bobbin case, with drop-in, see-through bobbin.

The tension of the thread is controlled by a tiny screw on the tension spring. Very few machines have numbered bottom tension. Many of the superb new machines have pre-set automatically controlled bottom tension that it is impossible to alter without upsetting the machine. However, the worker needs to be able to alter the bottom tension, to achieve decorative effects and to use thicker or metallic threads wound on to the bobbin by hand.

The answer to this is the remov-able bobbin case. This is fixed vertically, either to the left or centre front. The bobbin slots into the case, a catch prevents it from dropping out, and it is fitted into the race where it clicks home. Buy a separate bobbin case, mark it, and keep it for machine embroidery. Alter the tension on this bobbin case, keeping the original one for dress-making.

You cannot use twin needles with a side-loading bobbin case. These are easier to fit as they can be seen while the work is in progress, unlike the central bobbin case which is often hidden by the extension table (one manufacturer has incorporated a see-through panel), but the practised embroiderer can fit these by feel. A separate bobbin-filling method is preferable. You may need to change bobbins often.

Machines in the higher price range are superbly built. They are finely adjusted and sew beautiful, even stitches. Whatever the make, they do not take kindly to thick threads in the bobbin. If you wish to do free embroidery of this type, choose a machine in the middle price-range that has more tolerance between the needle and needle race, even if you have to sacrifice quality of stitching.

Machine manufacturers
Bernina
Brother
Elna
Frister Rossmann
Jones
Necchi
New Home
Pfaff
Singer
Toyota
Viking

Fabrics, threads and finishes

Before you start any machine embroidery, see that you have all the correct tools and attachments to hand. A good supply of bobbins, ready wound and kept in a see-through case, is a great help with frequent changes of bottom thread. Needles should be straight and sharp. Blunt or crooked needles are often the cause of missed stitches, or complaints that the machine will not sew properly. Make sure the machine is clean and well oiled.

Threads
All normal machine sewing threads can be used for machine embroidery. Sylko or cotton can be used top and bottom, but some synthetic threads are not quite so sympathetic. Threads ideal for stretch-stitching in dressmaking can be difficult to use. Some threads are made specially for machine embroidery. These have a special twist and a lovely silky sheen. Clark's Anchor machine embroidery thread is excellent and comes in two thicknesses, no. 30 and no. 50. The no. 50 is fine, and cheaper to use than ordinary cotton as it goes so much further. No. 30,

the thicker thread, looks lovely and gives a more textural line, but does not go so far. DMC also make excellent machine embroidery thread. The colours are rather more subtle than those of the Anchor range, but DMC is not so easy to obtain. Anchor can be found in most large department stores and specialist needlework shops.

If your machine will take thick threads in the bobbin, make sure they are smooth and not hard. Rough, hairy threads will catch on the needle race and could damage the machine. You can use perlé threads, fine crochet cottons, flat lurex, metallic cords sold for machine work, thin Twilley's gold-fingering in a variety of metallic colours, several strands of stranded embroidery silk or cotton; also reels of rayon floss which now take the place of silk floss and are very economical in use.

In the machine needle, working from the top, you can use silversmith or goldsmith. These are fine metallic cords which work well both for straight stitching and swing-needle work, provided satin stitches are not set too close. Soft, thick threads can be sewn down on top of the work, using zigzag or straight stitch. Hard cords or string should not be pierced by the needle, but zigzagged over.

Fabrics
Materials and backgrounds for working on should not be too closely woven. The machine needle cannot easily pierce harsh furnishing fabric, glazed cotton or fabrics with special finishes, or fabric painted or printed with fabric dye, so avoid these. Very shiny, slippery or extremely thin fabrics are difficult for the beginner to use. Any jersey or stretch fabric will stretch even more when put into the embroidery frame. Use only small pieces for appliqué. Cotton, cotton and synthetic mix or cotton poplin are ideal for the beginner working free embroidery. Thin, untextured furnish-

ing fabric, or a thicker fabric such as hessian that has a fairly open weave, can be used under the foot. Keep to single-colour, plain materials. Patterns and textures only confuse, unless they are incorporated as part of the embroidery design.

Experienced workers may like to try other fabrics such as leather, suede, suede-cloth, velvet, fur fabric or PVC. Velvets and suedes mark easily. When working free embroidery the frame can leave a ring mark. Sometimes this can be steamed out over a boiling kettle; if not, plan to work only small areas or motifs. A roller foot (an 'extra') can help with some of these fabrics.

All kinds of net can be used, single or double. Strong, white or coloured nylon net is easy to frame, does not tear and works well for free embroidery. Small pieces are useful in appliqué work. Even vegetable bags and nets can be used. Organdie, both cotton and nylon, is very effective worked in layers with parts cut away.

Backings
Satin stitch tends to pucker fine materials, in which case it is necessary to back the fabric first. You can use vanishing muslin, but this is not always obtainable. Although it can be ironed away when the work is complete, it is better to tear it off as the iron can damage the fabric, especially if it is synthetic, as well as melting away the backing. For embroidered pictures or panels, cushions or pockets on children's clothes, use thin iron-on material. All embroidery tends to stiffen the fabric, and any iron-on backing even more. So use this method with discretion. Some people prefer a thin muslin lining, tacked to the upper fabric; but unless this is perfectly framed, the two can pucker.

It can help to put thin paper behind the fabric when working satin stitch under the foot, and when using certain automatic patterns. You can use any of the following:

thin typing (copy) paper, strong tissue paper, paper kitchen towels, or coloured toilet tissue when working on pale-coloured fabrics. Most is torn away after the work is completed, but it is impossible to remove it all from under the stitchery. Soft tissue will disappear in washing. None of these methods is entirely satisfactory. It means that the stitch chosen is not really suitable for the material. Try out a different method of embroidery, or be prepared to frame your material and at the same time work under the foot. This means that you have to take the foot off to insert the frame under the presser foot bar and then replace it, but it does result in perfect satin stitch.

All kinds of fabrics may be used for appliqué, providing they do not stretch too much. Felt gives an almost quilted effect, fur fabrics and bouclé weaves add texture, and a restrained amount of shiny or glitter fabric adds highlights. Thicker materials may be held by a modicum of fabric adhesive before sewing down or you can use Bondaweb or a textile sealing powder that sets under heat from the iron. Do not have the iron too hot or you may damage some fine or synthetic fabrics.

Design

Make or adapt your own designs if you can; otherwise trace something, just a simple outline, and use that as a basis for embroidery. Nine times out of ten, your work will end up quite unlike the original tracing and you will have produced something of your very own. There is no harm in copying, so long as you are honest with yourself.

One very simple method is to take a leaf, preferably with well-defined indentations, and draw round it with a felt pen on grease-proof or typing copy paper. The outline can either be cut out and used as a pattern, or the paper can be placed on the material and the outline sewn through by machine,

either under the foot or freely in the frame. The needle perforates the paper which is torn away to leave the sewn pattern outlines. This method can be used with any traced designs. Keep it simple since too many lines confuse. You only need the main outlines and any strong divisions or design lines. It is much easier to work detail freely than to sew on top of a line. No one believes this until they have tried it. Fill in freely.

Alternatively you can mark the design outlines directly on to the cloth using dressmaker's carbon or tracing paper. These can be bought in most shops that stock dressmaking accessories. Carbon paper is too messy. You can draw outlines round various shapes with dressmaker's pencil or tailor's chalk. It is possible to use pencil, but it must be hard, as soft lead will dirty your material.

Although it is sometimes necessary for appliqué work, it is best to avoid tacking the design, since the threads get caught up in the foot or the needle. The fabric can be held

down with adhesive as previously suggested, but this method is not suitable for fine fabrics. Design for appliqué can be worked out using coloured paper or the colour pages from magazines, which help to give different colour and tone values. These shapes can be used as patterns or templates for cutting out fabric pieces.

Colour ranges of fabric, or tones of one colour using different textures, can be selected. Drop or twist threads on to the background to get design ideas. When you are satisfied with the effect, either pin down or trace the positions before moving. The greater the variety of fabrics and threads you have to choose from, the easier it is. So collect bits and pieces of all kinds. Have some system for finding them. For instance, sort out all blue materials, or all velvets, or all nets. It is easier to sort out thicker and interesting threads into colours, greeny-blues in one plastic box, yellowy greens in another. But you will find your own system.

Start a scrap book and collect

1 *Stretching finished embroidery*

design ideas: Christmas and birthday cards, patterned wrapping paper, advertisements from magazines, post cards, pictures of animals, fish, trains, ships, flowers—whatever takes your fancy. You will use only a few of them, but they are there for inspiration.

Plan your designs for a specific purpose. Cushions should look good any way up. Tablecloth edges are mainly viewed upside down and need only a small amount of flat embroidery in the middle. For corners and repeats look into a handmirror held upright against the design. Make quarter designs, or a segment of a circle, and repeat to make a whole.

Pillowcases and sheets are best made with the embroidery confined to the ends or top hem. It is easier to embroider a dress with the paper pattern pieces outlined, but not cut out. This allows room for working in the frame. Patterned materials can be enhanced with machine embroidery, but you need to experiment, so always allow extra material for this. When working in the embroidery frame, plan your design in circular areas, or move the frame more often to achieve a balanced design.

Make piped edges, using your piping foot for a neater finish to cushions and tea cosies. Follow the instructions in your machine book or a dressmaking manual; but remember to wash the piping cord first in case it shrinks.

Hem garments, mats and tablecloths first, and then sew decorative borders over double cloth. This gives a better stitch. To press, place work face down over a soft, bulky cloth and iron using a damp cloth or a steam iron.

Embroidery worked in the frame needs stretching since machine work tends to draw up the fabric. Leave a surrounding area unworked so that it can be pinned out. All pictures and panels need stretching. It is impossible to iron them afterwards.

You will need a flat, wooden

A subtle hint of blue lurex adds an exotic touch to the Chinese bird, applied using a swing-needle machine.

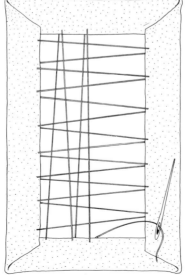

2 Mounting embroidery, back view

board, covered with several layers of newspaper and top sheet of blotting paper or white cloth. Dampen this with water sprinkled over. Stretch and pin out your embroidery, right side upwards, with drawing pins working from the centres outwards, and keeping the grain of the material straight (figure 1). Leave until the bottom layer of newspaper is bone dry before removing.

Pictures can be mounted over hardboard which is first covered with any soft, white cloth or a thin quilting wadding. The embroidery is placed on top of this and laced down the back on the wrong side of the hardboard. Lace first the sides, then the ends, working from the centres outwards (figure 2). Make sure the grain is absolutely straight before tightening up the lacing. Thin rayon cord or nylon knitting yarns or any strong thin thread can be used for this. Cover the back with material or paper glued in position.

Small pictures and Christmas cards can be glued down on to the back with fabric adhesive, but use it sparingly in order not to smudge the work.

Embroidery using a machine foot

Any line of machine stitching that does not hold two pieces of material together in a functional manner could be called embroidery. Lines of top stitching (even though they help give a firmer edge) and pin tucks come into this category; while rows of cording, lines of satin stitch and automatic patterns are truly decorative. Whether you have a simple straight-stitch machine, or a fully automatic model, you will be able to do some kind of embroidery.

Straight stitch machine
Start by thinking of your machine in terms of drawing or etching. The artist produces areas of light and shade simply by spacing out or drawing his lines closer together. Even denser areas are made by cross-hatching and these crossed lines in their turn can then be opened out. Take a pencil and have a go yourself. Now think of these lines in terms of machine stitching and try the same thing on your machine. At the end of your machined line, turn by lowering the needle into the cloth, raise the presser foot, swivel the cloth round the needle and lower the presser foot before sewing back the other way (figure 3).

Now try altering the stitch length lever. You can do this with your right hand while guiding the cloth with your left. Open and close stitches catch the light in different ways and and give an effect of texture.

The next variation is to alter the top tension. Have coloured thread in the needle and white thread in the bobbin. If you increase the top tension you will draw up more of the bottom thread and rows of white dots will show between the top stitches.

When both the top and the bottom stitches show evenly on both sides of the material you will know you have the correct tension. Always check tension on double cloth and write down the number for future reference.

Simple, curved lines can be worked with a straight stitch machine; but thin fabric may need backing with iron-on material. The fabric needs to be pulled round very gently while sewing. Do not try to do the work of the presser foot or the curves will be uneven. Have a light pressure on the foot, or use the half drop-feed position if your machine has this.

The next variation is to change the colour of the top cotton or use one of the reels of shaded thread made for machine embroidery. Determine the length of the colour change sequence of the thread and make use of this by starting at the lightest or the darkest part each time. This will produce a patterned effect.

You can use a variety of thread thicknesses in the needle, but be sure to use the correct needle size for the chosen thread.

Needle sizes
For no. 40 sylko or no. 30 machine embroidery thread, use no. 90 continental needle (old size no. 14). For no. 60 sewing cotton or no. 50 machine embroidery thread, use no. 75 or 80 continental needle (old size no. 11). For heavier thread, use continental no. 100 (old size no. 16).

It is possible to buy oversize needles for even thicker thread but it is just as easy to wind these threads round the bobbin, either by hand, or if the thread is in a reel or spool, some can be wound on in the normal manner using the bobbin winding mechanism. If the threads will not go through the tension device properly, by-pass this. Slip a pencil or a knitting needle through the hole in the spool of thread, and holding the protruding ends, let the thread wind on to the bobbin. You will find you can control the tension yourself. This is the method for winding on the flat lurex threads that must not be twisted.

Start by winding a few turns on the bobbin by hand. Place in posi-

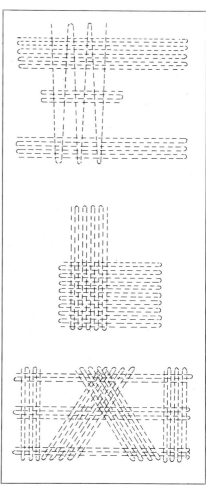

3 Patterns made by sewing straight stitches

tion on the machine for winding and with a pencil through the spool, untwist until the thread lies quite flat. Depress the foot control very gently in order not to wind too fast. Soft, thicker threads such as thick wool, perlé and stranded embroidery threads are better wound on by hand.

All thick threads are worked from the wrong side of the material, which means you cannot see the finished effect while you are working. But you can mark the design clearly on the wrong side of the material. Because the thread is thicker than normal, you will need to loosen the bottom tension screw so that the thread can pass through the bobbin-case tension spring. This

is where the advantage of having a separate bobbin-case comes in, leaving the unmarked bobbin-case for dressmaking. Use a touch of red nail varnish. Many people are nervous of altering the tiny screw as it can come out, and so can the tension spring, but provided that you always alter it over a box lid, it will not get lost. Although fiddlesome, it is not difficult to replace. It is best to alter

Persian bird worked from the reverse side with embroidery thread wound on to the bobbin.

(Bottom) Fine gold thread wound on to the bobbin and worked on the reverse gives highlight to the stem of the millet seedhead.

the screw only a quarter of a turn in any direction at a time. You have a small screwdriver in your tool box for this purpose. Clockwise tightens it up, anti-clockwise loosens it. Get to know the correct tension by feel. The thread should come out of the bobbin firmly. Try it before you alter it and make a sample of the correct tension on double cloth with a note of the top-tension number. When you have finished your embroidery, set the marked tension number on top and then reset the bottom tension until your second test sample is the same as the first.

Most machines with horizontal fixed bobbin-cases are easy to alter. Some even having a numbered bottom tension. Others are less accessible. On some bobbin-cases it is possible to by-pass the tension spring entirely. All this may sound a lot of bother, but the results are well worthwhile, and the use of thick and metallic threads enriches the stitchery.

Cable stitch

Thread the top of the machine with no. 30 machine embroidery thread or no. 40 sylko, and working from the wrong side of the fabric, first pull up the thicker bobbin thread by turning the balance wheel towards you by hand, and holding tightly on to the top thread, wriggle the thicker thread through to the surface. It is essential to have both threads on top of the work before starting. Have a medium stitch length and tighten the top tension slightly. The bottom thread needs to be pulled by the top thread at each stitch to give a pearl or cable effect. Work a test piece first and when you have sewn a few inches, turn over to see if the tension is correct and alter it if necessary. The procedure for metallic cords and lurex thread is the same. Use white or grey top thread for silver and orange, or yellow top thread to tone with gold. When mixing lines of straight stitch with cable, work the straight stitch first on the right

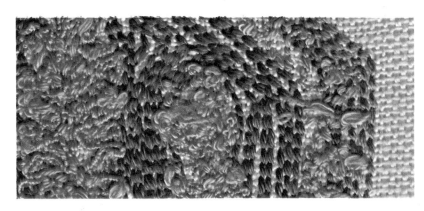

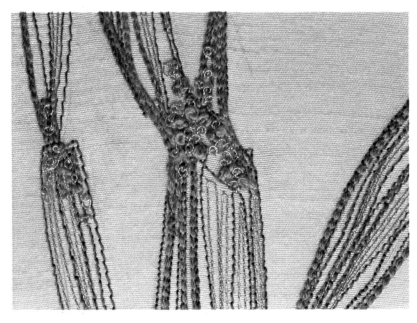

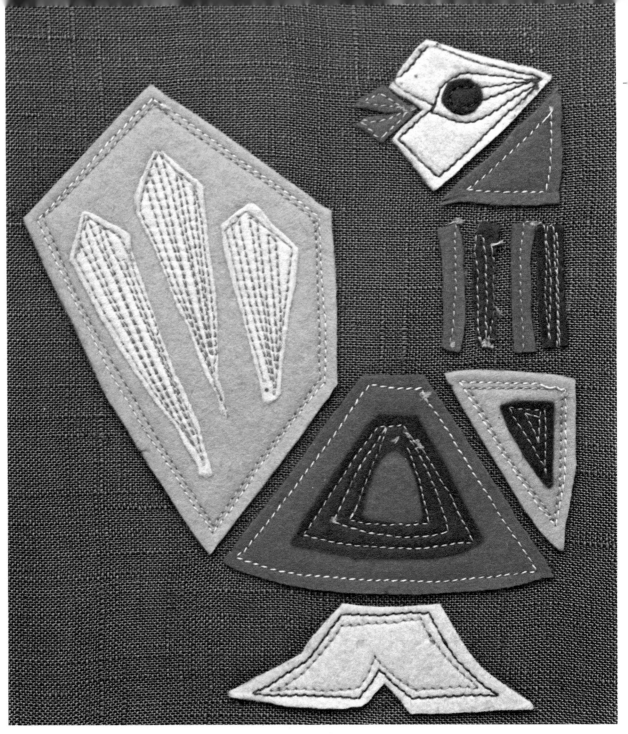

side, then turn over and work the cable from the wrong. Always add lurex and metallic cords last. These are the highlights and should be used sparingly.

Very thick, fluffy wool and slubbed bouclé threads can be applied by sewing down under the foot, using a fine top thread and medium stitch length. Anchor the thread first and hold so that it lies between the groove in the middle of the presser foot. Keep it taut and

hold it up a little.

Some machines have an attachment called the under braider. A plate with a ridged groove is screwed to the machine bed and the cord or braid threaded through the groove. The material is slipped under the foot and the design sewn from the upper but wrong side. Straight lines and curves are possible with sharp angles turned round the needle. This work can be done with thick quick-knit wool.

Birds of a feather. A basic design

Appliqué

You can machine over layers of net or organdie and then cut some layers away. Alternatively, small pieces of felt or material can be sandwiched between two layers of organdie and machined round. This turns brighter colours into pretty pastel shades, but remember that felt will not wash. Machining over felt gives a slightly indented, almost quilted, line and both felt and net are ideal for appliqué pictures as these materials do not fray. Larger areas of net can be applied over cut material to prevent fraying; but sometimes this effect can be used to enhance the textural quality of a picture, provided the material itself is held firmly before the edges are frayed.

Different layers of net give tonal value and applied thick threads add texture. Try sewing over suede or chamois leather using metallic cords. An ordinary needle will pierce the fine quality but you will need a leather needle for anything tougher.

Stylized bird

Increase the pattern size by drawing out on to a 2 cm grid. Trace off the outlines and transfer to card (figure 4). Number the shapes and cut out to use as pattern templates. If the picture is to be worked in appliqué, draw round the card patterns on

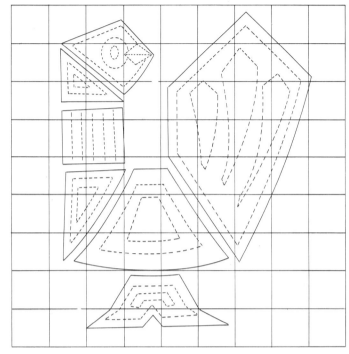

4 Basic pattern for appliqué birds

(Right) The head of the Egyptian bird in felt appliqué

(Far right) A more exotic treatment for the Chinese bird

(Below left) A layer of net for the stylish French bird

(Below centre) Bold colours for the Czech bird

(Below right) The Russian bird

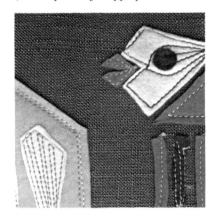

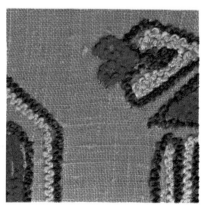

(Opposite) A balloon of felt appliqué floats across a sky of blue hessian.

The pilot stands in the basket while the burner above his head keeps him airborne. Felt pieces in the balloon picture were held in place with fabric adhesive before being stitched into position.

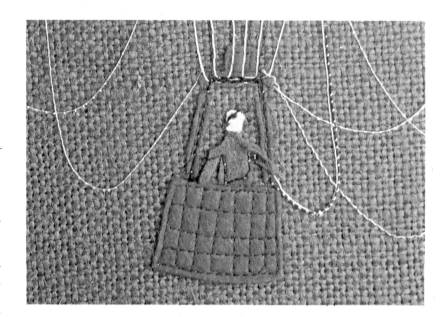

fabric or felt and cut out before applying to the background material. Felt pieces may be held temporarily with a spot of fabric adhesive, while other fabrics can be tacked in place.

If the bird is to be embroidered, draw round your card shapes directly on to the background material with a hard pencil or tailor chalk. The bird will sit inside a medium sized circular embroidery frame and does not need to be moved while working.

The balloon picture

Materials required: 0·5 m (22 in) blue/green hessian, one square of felt 23 cm² (9 in²) in each of the following colours: white, orange, red, light brown, dark green, mid-green, and light green; matching threads; a slightly thicker white cotton or thread; fabric adhesive; tracing paper.

Instructions for making the picture

Cut your hessian to measure 50 x 60 cm (20 x 24 in) on the grain of the material. Oversew the edges to prevent fraying. Work with a white thread in the bobbin throughout. Machine a guide line 5 cm (2 in) from the outer edge all the way round the hessian, keeping to the straight grain of the material. The finished picture size is 44 x 54 cm (17½ x 21½ in). The remaining material turns to the back when it is mounted.

Starting with the balloon, increase the size of your pattern by drawing on to a 2 cm (1 in) grid (figures 5, 6). Trace off the pattern and use this to cut up for individual pattern pieces.

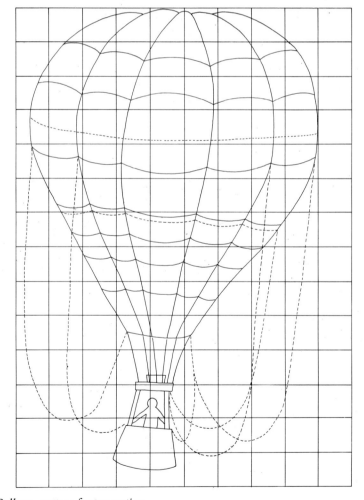

5 Balloon, pattern for top section

Write the colours on these and pin to coloured felt. Cut out smoothly and pin in position on to the background fabric. Hold down with just enough fabric adhesive to keep in place before machining round each piece, near the outer edge, with matching thread.

Next glue the basket in position and cut three narrow strips of felt for the framework that holds up the gas burner, which is represented by a small orange square. Machine with dark threads criss-crossing over the basket. The man is cut from a small green square, slit up the sides for the arms which are opened out. Make a tiny white blob for the head.

Return to the balloon and with a sharp pencil join up the lines from top to bottom following the indentations on the stripes. Machine down these lines to the top of the burner framework, using a dark thread. Decorate the horizontal bands of the balloon with contrasting thread.

Turn the work to the wrong side and with the thicker white thread in the bobbin, sew the supporting ropes from the white band of felt to the man's hand. This is the rope to release air from the balloon in descent. Pull all ends to the wrong side. Machine lighter ropes with thinner thread from the right side, easing gently round the curves. Machine the birds in position.

Trace off and cut out felt for the fields in a similar manner and place in position leaving approximately 1 cm ($\frac{1}{2}$ in) at the base and side clear of the edge stitching line. Machine in position in matching thread, overlap the central green hill over the brown one and leave gaps of background to represent the river. Machine lines to suggest a ploughed field, pull the ends through to the back and tie.

Finish by sewing a line of cable stitch over the guide line round the edge of the material working from the wrong side.

Swing needle machine
The side to side motion of the swing needle or zigzag machine adds width to the straight line. Some automatic embroidery stitches also make use of the reverse feed action producing circular stitch patterns.

A medium length stitch combined with a half-way swing produces zigzag stitch. Maintain the width, but close up the stitch length and you have satin stitch. Some machines have a fine adjuster for satin stitch. Machines with a vertical slotted stitch-length lever are less easy to adjust than the knob variety.

Do not set the machine too close for satin stitch. Too close (or too short) a stitch tends to pile up on itself and can snarl underneath. A controlled use of close satin stitch can be used to form raised blobs or blocks of stitches. But this is not for the beginner. Machines with three needle positions enable you to sew from the left, right or centre. If you start satin stitch from the left and work about 1 cm ($\frac{1}{2}$ in) in length, and then alternate straight stitch with satin stitch you get the pattern as in figure 7 (left); from the centre you get the pattern as in figure 7 (centre); from the right, the pattern is as in figure 7 (right).

Movement of the width lever while sewing produces lines of satin stitch in varying widths and it is possible with practice and rhythmic control to make your own embroidery patterns using a machine of the simple swing-needle type (figure 8), although most zigzag machines come with a selection of patterns. As with straight stitch sewing, designs can be made by crossing lines of zigzag or satin stitch (figure 9). Other effects are achieved by moving the stitch length lever to alter the density, opening up to zigzag and back again (figure 10).

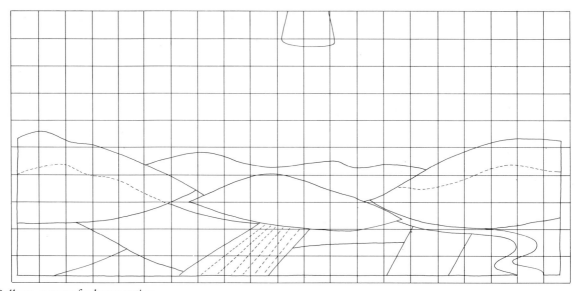

6 *Balloon, pattern for lower section*

The tension can be altered to show more or less of the bottom thread, which shows as a contrasting line on either side of the satin stitch. Shaded threads look especially attractive.

Try the effect of sewing over unusual fabrics such as felt, suede, layered net or even fur fabric. A roller foot may help. Experimenting can be fun and the results used on cushions, bags or garments.

Automatic patterns

These can be sewn in rows, or more freely in gentle curves, and look well when worked in metallic threads (sewn from the wrong side if thick) interspersed with rows of plain colour or shaded threads (sewn from the right side). Variety can be added by machining the patterns first from one direction and then back the other way. These rows can both face inwards or be worked back to back. Sew bought braid to material and border with rows of patterning or add patterns to plain ribbon bands. Vary the effect of striped material by embroidering some of the stripes and leaving others plain. Fine materials need backing with thin paper to be torn away; or Vilene which remains, but stiffens the fabric.

Some machines have a pattern elongator which alters the density and character of the stitch. Work a sampler of all your embroidery patterns, mark them and keep for future reference. This is especially useful when working embroidered pictures. Some patterns can suggest feathers or fish scales, wave form or all kinds of texture.

Applied threads

Zigzag stitch is used to hold thick threads on to the surface of the material. The needle does not pierce the thread but goes into the fabric on either side. For fine threads use a cording foot, available as an extra. This has a hole or slotted groove in the front of the foot into which the cord threads from front to back and is positioned ready for sewing. Have a ball of thread in your lap and hold lightly. There is no need to guide the thread as this is done by the foot. Corners need to be turned by pivoting round the lowered needle when the swing is on the inside of the curve.

Soft, thick threads such as wool can be zigzagged down without a cording foot. Anchor the thread by sewing when you start. Slubbed wools can be pierced by the zigzag at the thick parts, but try not to flatten and use a longer stitch. Cord or string can be held down by this method.

Have a matching fine thread in the top, and a colour to tone with the background in the bottom.

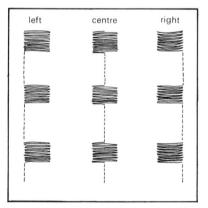

7 Alternating straight stitch with satin stitch

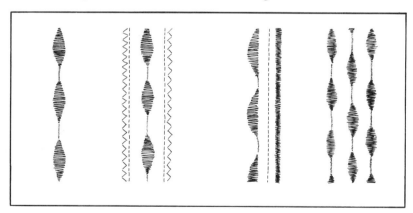

8 Moving width lever to form patterns

Roses round the door of a brightly coloured gabled house from the village.

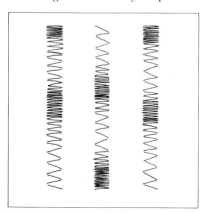

9 Crossing lines of satin stitch

10 Opening up stitch length lever

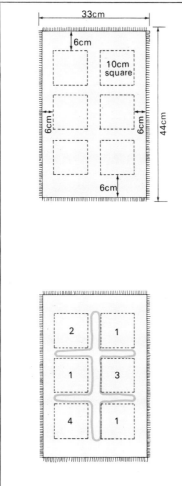

A swing needle has been used to overstitch the string in this design worked from the centre of the spirals.

11 Marking out string mat

12 Patterns for string mat designs

The tablemat illustrated was worked with string on a hessian ground, using a no. 50 machine embroidery thread in the top and no. 40 sylko in the bobbin. Cut out the pattern shapes in thin card, place in the desired order on the hessian and draw round the outlines with dressmaker's pencil or tailor chalk (figures 11, 12). Always work spiral designs from the outside to the centre. Sew once round your marked shape and then continue a presser foot width apart. A slight unevenness in width does not deter, but gives liveliness to the design. When you come to a corner, lower the needle into the cloth, raise the presser foot and pivot round easing the material so that the next zigzag stitch pierces almost the same place on the inside curve. Do not try to sew over the string or cord. Hold the cord fairly taut and slightly up,

in the direction you want to go, and machine along your chalk line or against your previous row of cording. Try out on spare material first and you will become more confident.

When you get to the middle, stop. Lift the presser foot and pull the string and the cotton and snip off leaving 2 cm (1 in). Thread the string through to the wrong side with a large-eyed needle. Also, pull the end of the lower thread in order to draw the top cotton through to the back.

Tie these ends together as zigzag stitch tends to unravel. To fringe the edges of the mat, work a line of zigzag stitch about 2 cm (1 in) from the edge, keeping to the grain of the material and then pull away the outer background threads to form a fringe. This is easier if you pull from the centre of the row.

Appliqué

Fabrics and threads can be applied to a background fabric for dresses, soft furnishings, wallhangings and panels. Large areas of applied fabric should match the grain of the background material, so that it will lie flat. But smaller pieces, up to 4 cm (1½ in) in length, can be placed at random. Applied fabrics on a dress need to be neatened well, with firm edges to withstand washing. Pin and then tack pattern pieces to the background before machining round the cut edges with a zigzag stitch (figures 14, 15). This should lie half on and half off the fabric edge. Match thread to your applied fabric and then sew with a satin stitch for a firmer edge. This line can be softened by rows of zigzag or straight stitch worked outside the applied edge. Keep shapes simple at first and use similar materials of a

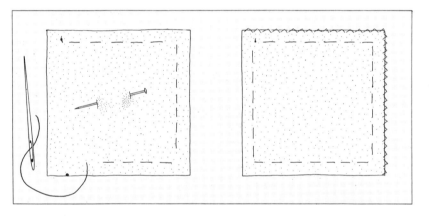

13 Tack position piece to background then overstitch using zigzag stitch

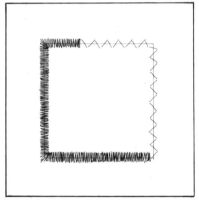

14 Satin stitch

A labyrinth of string, held by zigzag stitch, decorates a hessian place mat.

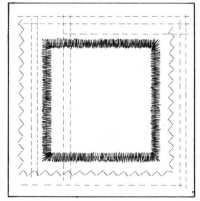

15 Soften outline with extra row of stitches

non-stretch type, avoiding slippery or easily frayed fabrics. These can be used to better advantage on wall panels, either for textural effect or backed with an iron-on material before cutting out for a firmer edge.

Fabric pictures

Choose simple design shapes to begin with. The picture, 'The Village', was worked by a 12-year-old girl. Children are less inhibited than adults and do not worry about perspective or straight, even lines. This adds charm to the work. A certain directness is essential to machine embroidery or the work can look laboured. The design for the houses was adapted from an illustration, but the church and churchyard are real. Fabrics suggesting the texture and pattern of the various buildings were cut out and tacked into place before holding down with a zigzag stitch, and later, satin stitch. Various automatic patterns suggest thatch or tiles and the trees were made by twisting bouclé wool around the fingers and then machining just to catch in places. Some hand stitches were added.

Reverse appliqué

This is another method where the design is machined through two or more layers of cloth and parts cut away to reveal different coloured levels beneath. Make sure the grain of the material matches throughout these layers. This is only suitable for small motifs and is best worked in an embroidery frame. (See method for free embroidery in next section.)

Fabrics applied to pictures or wall-hangings can be worked more freely with frayed edges, threads withdrawn, certain areas ruched; even the background cut away to reveal layers applied to the background. Decorative, thick threads can be laid on top, and beads and hand stitches added afterwards.

A delightful village scene designed and worked with imagination by 12-year-old Jane Thompson

The crazy patchwork cushion shows another use of applied fabrics and automatic patterns. The idea was adapted from the Victorian crazy quilts, fashionable in the 1870s and embroidered with herringbone and feather stitch. Twelve panels the size of the cushion could be joined together to make a bedspread.

First cut a backing of firm cotton, 7 cm (3 in) wider all round than the finished measurement of the cushion. The one illustrated measures 50 x 50 cm (20 x 20 in) and the velvet border is 3 cm (1¼ in) wide. Collect a variety of exotic fabric scraps. Velvet, rayon, terylene lining, brocade, saricloth, satin and lurex evening dress fabric were used for the cushion illustrated. All were left-overs from dressmaking, the odd-shaped pieces were chopped to a fairly even size, without altering the shapes and these were placed on

The Victorian passion for crazy patchwork and the abilities of the modern machine are combined in this richly composed cushion.

the background, starting in the middle and working outwards. Shapes overlap, nothing is cut away and the edges are not turned under. When you are satisfied with your design, pin in position and tack all to the background as flat as possible. This is important. Next, zigzag round the edges of the pieces of fabric using a toning thread. Next work your automatic pattern embroidery in contrasting threads, planning some stitches to face inwards and some to face outwards, or both methods on one patch. Choose patterns reminiscent of hand embroidery. Goldfingering or metallic cord outlines some of the patches, held down on the right side with zigzag stitch. The gold lurex thread is worked from the wrong side; you can see where to sew by using the zigzag outlines as a guide.

Sew a finishing border of black velvet round all four sides of the panel. This overlaps and hides all the rough edges of the patches. Work patterns round the border. Cut a backing for the cushion in black

velvet and machine the two sides together on the wrong side. This cushion cover cannot be washed and will need dry cleaning.

Embroidery without the machine foot
Free embroidery

By removing the foot and putting the feed out of action it is possible to sew in any direction with complete freedom. This opens up a whole new area of design possibilities, the embroidery varying not only in width of line, but in the variety of threads and textural effects. Some are achieved by altering the tension.

The wider line cannot be worked on a straight-stitch machine but this is compensated by the fact that many of the older machines can take thicker threads in the bobbin.

Free embroidery could be described as drawing with the sewing machine needle, except that it is the material which is moved, while the needle is fixed in position. To be able to move the material freely, the feed dog teeth must be put out of action. There are various methods of doing this. Modern machines have a knob or push-button that can be set to 'drop feed' or 'darning'. Some machines use a cover plate that fits over the teeth. This plate can be quite small and clip into holes on the needle plate; or it is interchangeable with the ordinary needle plate, but has a raised portion over the teeth; or it can fit under the needle plate and thus raise it up. Older machines have a screw underneath near the feed position. This is screwed into a different position, thus dropping the feed teeth, but see your instruction book for details.

If the machine foot is removed and the feed dog teeth put out of action there is nothing to hold the material down on to the machine bed and maintain the pressure necessary to be able to sew. This is the reason why the embroidery has to be worked on material tightly stretched into a tambour or circular

embroidery frame or hoop. This is made from two wooden rings, one inside the other; the outer is split and joined by a screw to tighten or loosen the pressure on the inner ring. This screw must lie horizontally or the frame will not slide on to the machine bed. If you bind the inner ring with bias-strip, bandage or bias-binding it will hold the material more firmly and be less likely to slip. Neaten finished ends on the inside of the ring. Do not bind too thickly, just enough to overlap.

Framing the material

Lay the inner ring flat on the table and place the material over this, wrong side uppermost. The outer ring is pushed down over this to enclose the cloth. Tighten the screw, and then invert the framed material so that it lies flat on the table, right side uppermost. To tighten the material pull the free edges of the cloth up over the outside of the frame and in towards the centre. When you tap the framed material with a finger, it should sound drum tight. Very slightly push the inner frame through the outer ring so that it protrudes just a fraction. This is to prevent the outer frame from catching on any ridges on the machine bed. All this only takes a few seconds to do with practice, but it is important if you wish the machine to sew properly. The flat side of your framed material lies on the machine bed and you work into the hollow, which is the right side.

Your frame can be anything from 10-31 cm (4-12 in) across; but 18 cm (7 in) is the most suitable size to begin with. The presser bar may catch against a small frame, and anything larger than 20 cm (8 in) will come up against the upright of the machine arm. Later you will learn how to position the larger frame by turning it round. Metal frames are not suitable as some are very deep, while in others there is not enough tolerance to allow for binding. Some manufacturers supply a frame as an optional accessory.

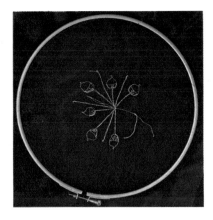

A frame is essential for free machine embroidery. Some machine manufacturers supply frames suitably designed for their specific model, however the traditional adjustable wooden frame is quite adequate for most requirements.

Working the embroidery

The most suitable material to start with is cotton poplin, or pieces of old sheeting for practice, provided the pieces are strong enough to stretch in the frame. Avoid thick or stretchy materials, or those with dressing in. Use a no. 90 needle and a correspondingly fine thread to start with; it is easier to sew. The bobbin thread can be similar or slightly thicker, but use a contrasting colour. You are now ready to begin, but first check the following points:

1 Remove the presser foot and screw. (Put into a box lid.)
2 Put the feed out of action.
3 Thread machine top and bottom and see there is plenty of thread in the bobbin.
4 Frame your material.
5 Set the machine for straight stitch.

To start, raise the needle to its highest position and place the framed material under the pressure bar. This can only be done if the presser bar is in the raised position. In some machines the gap is small and you may have to tilt the frame. If you started to sew now, you would have no top tension. It is essential to lower the presser bar lever as this controls the top tension.

The fact that the foot is removed makes no difference to the tension which is controlled separately.

Starting to sew

1 Lower the presser bar lever.
2 Lower the needle into the cloth, turning the balance wheel towards you by hand.
3 Make a stitch and draw up the bottom thread through to the surface of the material by pulling with the top thread. It is essential to have both threads on the surface of the material before you start.

Hold on to both thread ends and make two more stitches, turning the balance wheel by hand. This will lock your threads and when you have sewn 2-5 cm (1-2 in) they can be cut off close to the cloth. Start by holding the frame on either side keeping hands and fingers well away from the sewing area or you may pierce your finger with the needle. Provided you hold the frame correctly there is no danger of this.

Sew gently and move the frame slowly with a circular motion. The stitchery will follow this motion. Because the feed teeth have been put out of action they do not connect with the stitch length mechanism, so this no longer works. You yourself are the stitch length regulator. If you push the frame slowly under the needle, tiny stitches result. If you push it quickly, the stitches have less time to build up, and longer stitches result. Push the frame too quickly and the top cotton will break; push it too slowly and the bottom cotton will snarl up underneath. A few minutes practice will help you to move the frame evenly and smoothly and where you want it to go. Do not try to make any designs at first; just get the feel of it, sew in circles, backwards and forwards in any direction. It is said that it takes 20 hours work for a machine embroiderer to become at ease. So do not give up before then.

To finish, raise the presser bar, pull the threads in the normal way and cut off close to the work.

Straight-stitch machine embroidery will not come undone. In fact, one of the rules in this work is not to unpick. First, this is very difficult to do and leaves nasty holes where the needle has been. Secondly it is much easier to sew over mistakes, or incorporate them in the design. This method of embroidery is extremely fluid by its very nature. Try to keep it that way. You will find that you have to think quickly. Decide where you want to go before you start sewing, and then sew. This is much easier than trying to sew over drawn pattern lines. However, pencil dots are useful as points to aim for, and guiding lines for outlines only can be useful when working a larger design.

Not all your work will be small. At first you will have to remove the frame from under the machine when you want to move it to another area of cloth. But with experience you will find you can reframe on the machine by loosening the frame screw just a little and forcing the frame over the cloth in the new position.

Designs planned to be worked in a circle are easiest at first. Mark the centre of the area and any points to be aimed at round the circumference. A flowerhead would have one dot in the middle and one for each of the five petal points. An odd number of petals or leaves look better from a design point of view.

You will find it easier to control the work when the frame is pushed away, rather than towards you. This comes with practice, but you can always keep the needle lowered at the points and then turn round and machine the other way. Try to plan your designs as continuous lines. The same line can be sewn over again and again, provided it is not too thick. Use a smaller size embroidery frame for circular designs started from the centre. The size of the frame acts as a limit to how far you can sew and helps keep the design even. Control of the frame may require a little practice when using a free arm machine.

Satin stitch width lever

When you feel happy sewing thin lines, set the width lever to half way and try using a thicker line. This looks quite different. This method can be used for writing names, the

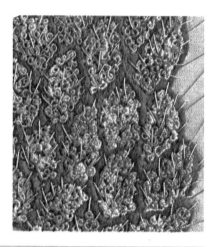

A millet seedhead with fine waving leafy strands of blue and gold thread. (Right)

The seedhead was worked separately in shaded whip stitch on a background of felt before being applied to the background cloth. (Below)

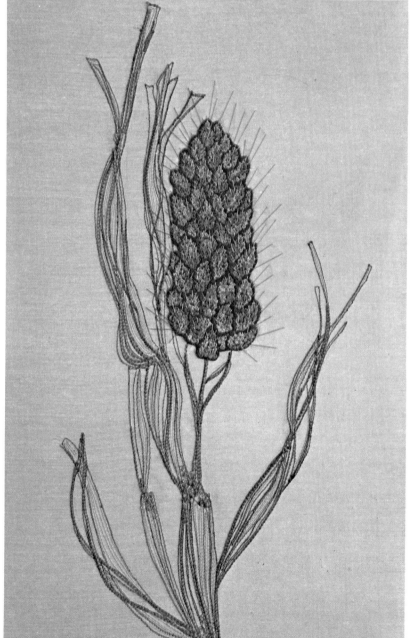

width of the stitch acts like the broad nib of a pen, and according to the angle, produces both thick and thin lines in the curves. The frame needs to be moved from side to side and up and down, but kept on the same plane.

Since you control the stitch length, the satin-stitch line will open up to zigzag when you push the frame more quickly. Do not let satin stitch build up or it will jam underneath. When you feel really confident, it is possible to control the frame with the left hand only and to alter the stitch width knob or lever with the right, while the machine is sewing. This works well for flower petals, leaves, or any flowing design.

The darning foot
The use of this foot is included under the heading of free embroidery as it enables you to sew freely and may help some beginners who are nervous when using the machine without a foot. With some machines, especially those with a raised type of cover plate, it is the only way to achieve satisfactory free embroidery. This is because the frame rocks over the protruding cover plate and needs the darning foot to hold the material down for a firmer contact. The disadvantages are that it obscures the work and that it can be used on its own only when sewing thicker, firmer or backed materials. Otherwise it has to be used in conjunction with the embroidery frame and this means fitting it after the frame has been slipped under the presser bar.

There are various kinds of darning foot, but the principle is the same: that the cloth can be moved when the needle and needle bar are raised, and that the cloth is held down into position when the needle and needle bar are lowered. Some models have a spring and others have a spring controlled arm that rests over the needle bar. The needle goes up and down very quickly while sewing and this enables the worker to move

the cloth at will. Use the dropped feed position. Some machines include this foot with the accessories. One firm makes a foot that will fit several types of machine, and can be bought in large department stores. Do not ask for an embroidery foot. You may be offered a see-through plastic presser foot which is a help when sewing satin stitch or automatic patterns.

Adding texture to straight-stitch sewing
Whipped stitch Set the machine to straight stitch and thread with a contrasting colour in the bobbin. Tighten the top tension so that the colour from the bottom thread comes to the top and whips round the top thread. The tighter the top tension, the more it will whip round. However, there is danger that the top thread will break, so it may be easier to alter the bottom tension screw. The whipped effect can be varied by pushing the frame faster or slower. Slower and the bottom colour builds up; faster and it is more opened out and the top thread shows through. This can be used to create a lovely textured effect, especially when lines are worked close together.

Exaggerated whip stitch This is sometimes called feather stitch. Loosen the bottom tension until large, spiky stitches from the bottom thread form over the top thread to create a feathery effect. This is best worked in circles, pulling the top thread gently round and letting the spiky stitches build up in some places and open out in others. This adds texture to plainer areas or can be used on its own. Sew spaced sequins on to the collar or yoke of an evening dress and embroider feather stitch round the sequins. This will have to be worked before the pattern pieces are cut out, or mounted temporarily on a larger backing in order to hold in the embroidery frame.

Free cable stitch Except that it is worked freely in the frame, this is the same as cable stitch worked

under the foot. It is always worked from the wrong side using thick threads wound round the bobbin. Try to keep the machine at an even speed and avoid jerky movements. Curved shapes need to be sewn with a definite pull as you go round. When the work is finished, all thread ends, thick and thin, must be pulled through to the wrong side and tied off securely.

The framed panel, millet seedhead, was sewn mainly in cable stitch, using Clark's cotton à broder and stranded silks with metallic cords. It was worked in the frame which had to be moved several times. Main design lines were pencilled in on the wrong side and the stalks and leaves worked first. The seedhead was worked separately in shaded whipped stitch on felt, cut out and applied to the background afterwards. Some hand stitches were added using the metallic cord for French knots and straight stitches.

Rayon floss thread is excellent for free cable stitching and works well on velvet. Try flowers in the floss outlined with metallic cord. This will only be suitable for small designs as the velvet marks in the frame. Metallic cords and goldfinger look very rich, especially when worked on dark backgrounds. The Paisley Indian pine cone motif on the patchwork bedspread illustrated was first drawn as a simple shape in tailor chalk on the wrong side of the material. The outline was sewn round once, and then twice again inside the shape.

Finally, the loops or scallops were worked round the outside (figures 16, 17). Thinner metallic cords can be added to areas of whipped stitch worked in variegated threads. These small, embroidered motifs can be used in a variety of ways. Mount them behind cut-out card for birthday or Christmas cards or mount on thin card and glue behind a glass paperweight. You could use them on pockets, decoration on a dress, or you could use all your worked samples to make a patchwork bed-

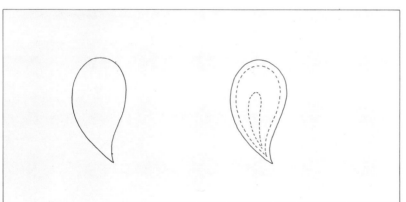

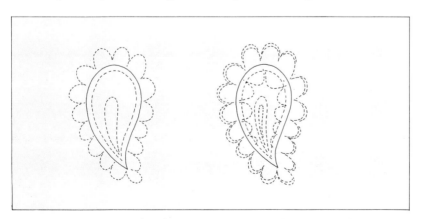

16 *Paisley Indian pine cone design, outlined by machine using thick silver thread*

Silver Paisley Indian pine cone on a background of deep green poplin.

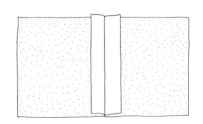

17 *Scallops round outer edge of pine cone design, with thinner cord added to centre and outer scallops*

18 *Patchwork bedspread—machine two patches together on wrong side*

By limiting the number of background colours, the effect of different embroidery stitches and patterns is emphasized in this crisp cotton bed cover.

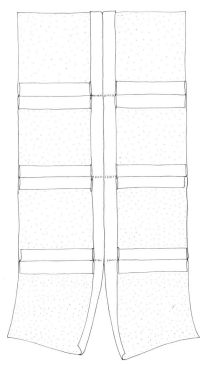

19 Machine rows of patches together, open out and press

spread that would be really individual.

Patchwork bedspread

Limit your colours to a definite colour scheme. This will add unity to the great variety of processes you may wish to try out. The background materials in the bedspread illustrated are all cotton poplin, and the colour scheme kept to white, yellow, greens and silver. Work several motifs on one larger piece of material before cutting up into patches. The finished size of the patches is 10 cm (4 ins) square. Cut a piece of strong card to this size to use as a template. Place over the motif, wrong side, and draw round in pencil. Seam allowances of 1 cm ($\frac{3}{8}$ in) must be added afterwards. Cut out, pin together by the pencil lines, then seam together along these lines (figure 18). Rows of patches can then be sewn together (figure 19).

Spread a sheet on to a bed and lay out and plan your patch positions on this before sewing. It is much easier to judge the finished design this way. Pick up each row of patches in the correct order and stack ready for machining together. Line the bedspread with cotton material and finish with a border 10 cm (4 in) wide plus seam allowances, using one of the darker colours for this (figure 20) which will make an effective surround and set off the colours of the patches.

Working on net and organdie

Floss threads can be sewn on to layers of net, so can thin metallic cords. In fact you can sew on most kinds of net, including plastic bags so long as the needle catches on to the threads if they are far apart. Frame single layers of net carefully. At first it will feel strange to see the needle plate through the net but you soon learn to ignore this. Mark your design centres with a pin and start sewing continuous designs from the centre. It is necessary to bring both threads through to the top before you start. Flowers sewn on net can be cut out and then used in layers to simulate free-standing petals. Secure the centre with pearls or crystal beads, mount them on a bridal headband or use them to add a touch of elegance and distinction to an evening dress.

Layers of organdie can be sewn together and one layer cut away. In places, all layers can be cut away and the resulting hole sewn over with a very steady, even stitch to catch on to the other side and come back again like a spider's web, twisting round the centre and back to the outer edge. This is machined cut work.

The organdie can be mounted on net and a design sewn through both layers. Afterwards, parts of the organdie layer are cut away to leave the net and form a design of light and shade. This method was used

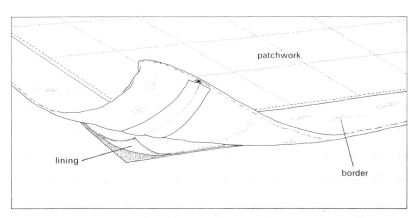

20 Sew border to patchwork and lining, fold seam allowances under and hem to lining by hand

for the picture of Briar Rose's Palace in the 'Sleeping Beauty' picture. You need a pair of fine sharp scissors and a very steady hand, as one slip would cut the net beneath. Just one or two design lines were lightly pencilled on to the organdie, including the stalks of the roses, and the flower centres as dots. The rose design was drawn from a rambler rose and stylized to fit the circular pattern. The embroidery was mounted over a blue satin background before the picture was framed.

Thick threads

These can be applied freely to the surface of the material using free straight stitching. The beginner would be well advised to use a darning foot as the threads need to be held down fairly near the exposed needle. The picture adapted from a postcard reproduction of Van Gogh's 'View of Arles' was worked this way. Do not set out to copy anything exactly, but try to recreate the mood of a picture in fabrics and threads. The Van Gogh was started by winding various slubbed weaving threads across the fingers to achieve the texture of the trees, laid on to the fabric and sewed down immediately before the effect was lost. The background fabric was woollen dress material and was worked without the frame. Whisps of mohair were twisted round the fingers and lightly sewn down for the fruit trees. The clouds and water reflections were worked freely in shaded crochet threads, using the colour change sequence to advantage. The main part of the picture was worked very directly and this is the best approach for pictorial work to obtain a good representation.

Optional extras and additional processes

Many machine manufacturers supply a variety of extras in the form of attachments, special feet and needles. As a general rule, these are

made to fit the machine they are intended for; but some are interchangeable and it is worthwhile finding out just exactly what will fit your machine. They are made to achieve decorative effects not easily obtainable by other methods. Included are twin and triple needles, wing or hemstitch needles, eyelet stitchers, a variety of circular and spiral stitchers, and the darning and braiding feet already mentioned.

Twin needles

These will fit machines that thread from front to back. Two needles, side by side, share a single shank at the top that fits in the normal manner. Push up hard and tighten the screw. There are two reels of thread on top and one thread in the bobbin beneath. Machines suitable for twin needlework will have two thread reel supports, side by side, and some have two sets of thread

machine instruction book and follow the recommended threading.

Hold the threads from both needles and turn the balance wheel by hand to bring up the single bottom thread. You may need a looser top tension as the top threads share the bottom thread and form a kind of zigzag on the wrong side. Straight stitch produces parallel lines of stitching.

The thread can be the same in each needle, or you can contrast in colour or fine metallic cord. If you use twin needles in conjunction with a buttonhole foot, or any foot that has a wide space in the middle, the parallel lines will be pushed up to form a ridge or tuck. Some machines have a cording device with a grooved plate fixed in front of the needles so that a cord can be enclosed beneath by the needles. It is possible to sew over a cord held taut under the material.

Sewing round corners can present a problem and have to be eased round in three stages, turning the balance wheel by hand, since you cannot pivot round twin needles. Some machines have triple needles, sewing three parallel lines at once.

Zigzag stitch and certain patterns can be sewn but the swing has to be reduced because the double needle takes up more room. Patterns suitable for twin needlework will be marked either in your instruction book or on the machine. A three-step zigzag looks attractive and so does the blind hemmer stitch. Several linear stitches such as curves and scallops double up well. When set to satin stitch, and using the normal presser foot the effect is flatter and can be very decorative when two separate shades of thread are used as they merge together in places.

Change over the threads to try different effects, or use silversmith or goldsmith in one of the needles.

Rows of stitching can cross at right angles, and shallow curved lines are possible, but this tends to distort the fabric if it is pulled too hard when sewing on the cross.

Winged or hemstitching needles

These needles have a broad, flat wing of metal protruding at either side and tapering to the needle eye. They are used to make decorative holes in material like organdie or fine, close cotton. Synthetics are not suitable as the holes close up again.

Sew a row of zigzag stitch and then back again, letting the needle slip into the holes of the previous row. If your machine is likely to creep, pull the cloth slightly to correct this tendency. Patterned areas can be built up like this.

The twin winged needle, or hem stitching needle, has a winged needle at the left and a plain one on the right. Rows of zigzag stitch or blind hemming stitch can meet to share the middle holes. Thread can match the organdie background, or contrast, or a plain and contrast can be threaded up. These needles are expensive. However, they are worth experimenting with since they produce very decorative embroidery on fine, natural fabrics suitable for

Leafy vines twist round the turrets of the castle. The organdie is carefully trimmed to shape after stitching has been completed, using very sharp scissors.

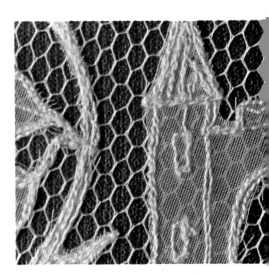

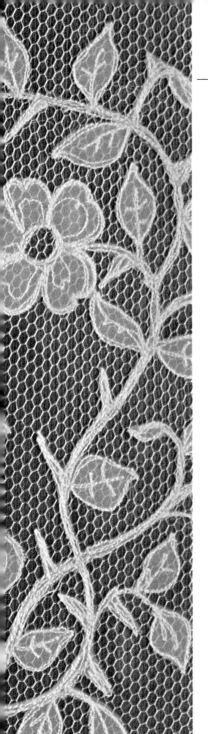

A palatial residence of fine organdie for Sleeping Beauty, on a background of net.

guides to prevent the threads from twisting.

In most of the simpler machines the two threads are treated as one until they separate at the final thread guides above the needle. In others the threads are divided at either side of the top tension discs but see your

table mats, handkerchiefs, blouses and decorative edgings for dresses or lingerie.

The chain stitcher
Some machines with a removable front loading bobbin case have an interchangeable chain stitching device which takes the place of the bobbin and bobbin case. The needle is threaded from the top and about 20 cm (8 in) thread is pulled through the eye. There is no bottom thread, as the chain stitch forms underneath on the wrong side of the material. Set for straight stitch, a medium stitch length and adjust the top tension carefully to give the correct chain shape. Too tight will distort, and too loose will be loopy. Chain stitching works best in straight lines. Corners need to be turned as a gentle curve, avoiding sharp angles or the chain thread will break. Neaten off by hand or it will unravel.

Eyelet stitcher
This takes the form of an alteration to the needle plate. Some machines have a removable eyelet plate that is substituted for the ordinary needle plate. Others have a small, clip-on plate that covers the feed teeth. Both

Airy green and white bubbles of zigzag float across a green patch, worked with a flower stitcher and shaded thread.

have a small, slotted circle of metal protruding above the needle hole. The fabric is pierced with a stiletto, or an awl, and the resultant hole is fitted over the metal circle. Set the machine to stitch width 2 to 4 mm ($\frac{1}{12}$-$\frac{1}{6}$ in), stitch length to 0, and remove the presser foot. Stretch the material in a frame and fit the eyelet hole over the metal circle. Lower the presser bar and revolve the embroidery frame round the eyelet while the machine is sewing. The needle dips into the slot and binds the eyelet with a close satin stitch. You can sew round a second time to produce a thicker eyelet, but turn the frame more quickly to space out the stitches.

Flower stitcher
Eyelets can also be made on the flower stitcher, but they are not true eyelets, the holes having to be pierced afterwards. The flower stitcher is a small circle stitching device, used mainly in conjunction with automatic patterns to produce small circular flowers. It is fitted in place of the presser foot. A bar rests over the needle clamp, which is raised and lowered with the needle and clicks into a series of grooves set round a circular plastic plate. The machine is set to darn and presser bar pressure adjusted. A screw adjusts the needle position in relation to the centre of the circle, enabling you to sew smaller or larger

circles, and to vary the size of the inner circular area.

Material needs backing with vanishing muslin or thin paper. These can be torn away afterwards. Do not make the central hole too small or the circular stitching may creep as you sew round. Start with a few straight stitches to lock the thread and end in a similar manner. There is no need to remove the material when working in a new position but leave long enough threads so that they do not catch or distort underneath.

To set for flower stitching choose any pattern or cam that does not involve reverse feed action and use a width from 2 mm ($\frac{1}{12}$ in) upwards. If used with the correct machine, it is set so that the number of grooves can be divided by the number of stitches in each pattern repeat, or motif, always producing five pattern sets, or petals. Central position is altered by moving the ring and the cloth at the same time. There is no need to cut the thread. A flower centre can be the same as the outer petals, but in a smaller version, or a different pattern setting. These flowerheads look well with free machine embroidery added, using the satin stitch width lever to make stalks and leaves. (See patchwork bedspread.)

The spiral stitcher
This is similar to the flower stitcher

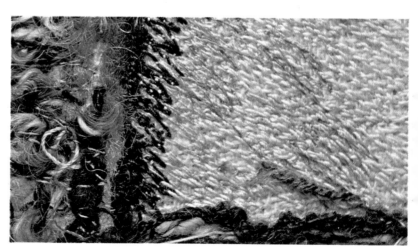

A new look for Van Gogh. A machine embroiderer's interpretation of 'The View of Arles'.

(Left) A detail of the 'View of Arles' shows how thick threads can be applied using free straight stitching, contrasting well with the smooth background of sky.

and also uses a lever over the needle bar to move a series of grooves set in a circle. It works on the spirograph principle; two circles, moving one inside the other to produce circular but off-centred patterns. However, instead of moving a pencil as the toy, the machine needle is fixed and the spiral stitcher moves round it. The material is stretched in a special frame that has cogged teeth on its inner circle which fit into the teeth on the stitcher. There are five positions for pattern settings and further alteration is possible by placing the needle at left, right or centre. There are two different sized circles to stretch the cloth in, one giving a nine pointed pattern and the other nineteen. If you add zigzag width, automatic patterns and twin needles, the design possibilities are endless.

Two colours of thread in twin needles look very decorative especially if one is in silver or gold. Some experimentation with size is necessary when using automatic patterns to give the best result from the repeat. The results can be surprising.

The circular motifs can be used to decorate handkerchief corners, table linen, dresses or can be mounted behind circular cut-out card to make excellent birthday and Christmas cards.

Circular stitcher

This is for sewing circles with a radius of 3-13 cm (1-5 in) either using straight stitch, zigzag, automatic patterns or twin needles. It is useful for decorating table mats, cushions, and children's clothing. Overlapping circles can border curtains or repeat the central pattern on a bedspread.

A metal arm with an adjustable length, marked for measuring, screws and slots into the two holes in the machine bed to the right of the needle plate. The other end of the arm terminates in a spike that holds the material in position, topped with a screw. The material revolves around this screw so that a constant circular line is sewn under the foot. The distance between the spike and the presser foot determines the size of the circle. This is an easy attachment to use. Circles can be overlapped or worked inside one another to form the design.

Rug or carpet forks

These vary, but basically they have two prongs around which threads are wound. Using straight stitch and the presser foot, a line is machined between the prongs while the fork is gradually withdrawn from the loops. More thread can be wound on before the last loops have been sewn down so that continuous strips of loops can be sewn in place on the backing material. These loops can be left as they are, or they can be cut to form a tufted fabric. The lines can be sewn close together or apart, depending on the desired effect.

All kinds of threads can be used from thick rug wool to fine embroidery thread provided they can be pierced by the needle. A natural hessian makes a good backing for rugs, and any furnishing fabric for cushions decorated with separate lines of tufted stitching.

The following are not necessarily special attachments, but different uses for various feet.

The tailor tacking foot Some machines are provided with this foot which has a metal blade fixed between the two arms of the presser foot so that a zigzag stitch forms a raised loop over the blade. This is used for tailor tacking and the raised loops are cut to provide guide lines in dressmaking. It is set at a stitch width of approximately 2·5 mm ($\frac{1}{10}$ in) and a longish stitch length. If you set the machine to satin stitch, the loops build up to form a thick, looped line of thread and can be used for decoration, either cut or left as they are. Effective in shaded thread, the loops can be sewn in lines, or in spiralling circles on firm or backed material. The lines can be apart or close together to form a thick, towel-like fabric. It is essential to back the finished work with iron-on material as the loops are not fixed and would otherwise pull out.

The darning foot This can be used for embroidered free quilting, either as a continuous linear design or over patterned material, following the pattern outlines. Medium sized floral prints work well. Tack your top material, synthetic quilting wadding and thin backing together with basting stitches by hand, starting from the centre and working outwards.

Work with the feed teeth down, or better, at half-dropped feed if your machine has this position. Hold the layers of fabric firmly and move under the foot as you would the embroidery frame, following the outlines of the pattern freely, but not necessarily exactly, to achieve an all over patterned effect. Have a pair of small scissors handy to snip your tacking threads as these are likely to catch on the foot.

If you prefer to decorate plain fabric, draw your design on the wrong side and work from that side. All ends must be drawn through to the back of the work.

This quilted fabric can be cut up and made into tea cosies, oven gloves, needlecases, squab cushions, bedcovers or can also be used on garments.

Feather stitch This is not the same as the exaggerated whip stitch but is so called because of the feathery effect. It is worked in the embroidery frame, with the zigzag foot added afterwards and either with the feed up or in half drop feed position. Set to satin stitch and width from 2 upwards. Sew, and at the same time, swing the frame from side to side. This provides the feathery effect. The faster you move the frame, the more spiky it will become. Try not to cross over your lines or the result will be muddled.

All of these attachments need care and patience in setting up. But once correctly set, they can save a great deal of time. They are extremely effective, they can be combined with other types of machine or hand embroidery and they give a great deal of enjoyment to the user.

Suppliers of embroidery materials

Anchor and DMC threads	Mace and Nairn, 89 Crane Street, Salisbury, Wiltshire SP1 2PY
	Mary Allen, Wirksworth, Derbyshire, DE4 4BN
	Christine Riley, 53 Barclay Street, Stonehaven, Kincardineshire AB3 2AR
Lurex and metallic threads	Mace and Nairn, 89 Crane Street, Salisbury, Wiltshire SP1 2PY
	Stephen Simpson Ltd, Avenham Road Works, Preston PR1 3UH
goldsmith and rayon floss	Silverknit Yarns, The Old Mill, Epperstone By-pass, Woodborough, Nottingham NG14 6DH

For bold effects
- or exquisite details

Stitched rugs are not only enormously adaptable but they are also most exciting additions to home decor. In the following pages the basic techniques are all thoroughly and simply explained, design ideas are suggested complete with instructional details. From rich, shaggy Scandinavian rugs in vivid colours to intricate and delicate oriental contrasts, from tiny details that can be exquisitely rendered to the broad bold effect, rug making is a splendidly satisfying skill.

New scope for an ancient skill

The making of carpets and rugs goes back many centuries. Most people are familiar with rugs from the East with their beautiful designs and colouring. The different countries and districts had their own styles and patterns. The Persians favoured flowing curves while the Turks preferred more geometrical designs. These were all made on looms, the warp being set up at the beginning and the weft and pattern added as the work progressed.

Rugs can, of course, still be made on a loom, but this method requires a good deal of space. Other methods of rug making have developed over the years. Some use canvas, and a great many people have made rugs with a latchet hook and short lengths of thick rug wool on a fairly coarse canvas. While this makes satisfactory rugs, the use of finer canvas and wool offers greater scope in terms of design. The final results can not only be very beautiful indeed, but also produce a satisfying reward for the labour expended on it.

Rugs made using the last method can be worked at a table or while sitting comfortably. The tools required can all be found in the normal work basket. The designs need not incorporate motifs from traditional rugs, though many transplant well into the modern idiom. In addition to this obvious source, it is surprising how many patterns can be found in unexpected places, such as carvings, stained glass windows, mosaics, and various textiles. In fact, a wealth of inspiring ideas for designs can be found by the discerning eye.

In comparison with many leisure activities, rugmaking need not be an expensive craft. Once the basic stitches have been mastered, a rug can be made which will enhance the home and give lasting satisfaction. It might make a present, incorporating in the design something which will make it personal to the recipient.

Materials

Canvas

One of the best canvases to use for this type of rugmaking is that having a double thread in each direction for both the warp and the weft. It comes in a variety of widths and is usually readily available from craft suppliers. Canvases are graded according to the number of holes per 2·5 cm (1 in), therefore 5s canvas has five holes to every 2·5 cm (1 in) measure. This is the most useful grade for beginners as the work progresses fairly quickly and the holes are sufficiently close together for a satisfactory design. Ordinary tapestry needles are used, size 16 for this canvas, with two threads of wool for pile and most of the flat stitches.

A coarser grade of canvas, which is also available in several widths, is 4s. This is used for the shaggy Scandinavian Rya-type rugs. With this grade, a size 12 needle and four threads of wool for the pile stitch are best. Both these canvases are made of stiffened cotton and are quite satisfactory for general rugmaking, but for finer work it is better to use a foreign-made linen canvas. The 8s cotton canvas loses

The size of needles suggested is a guide only. Provided that the needle and the wool can be pulled easily through the canvas, it does not greatly matter, and sometimes a finer or coarser size may be easier.

Wool

The most commonly used wool for this work is a 2-ply Axminster carpet wool, available from carpet factories. This normally contains a percentage of nylon and is moth-proofed, so catastrophies apart, a rug made from it should last for many years. It is pleasant to work with and one thread or more can be used to produce the thickness required.

There are several different ways of buying it. The cheapest is as thrums. This word has a long history but has now come to mean the left-overs from carpet factories. Mixed thrums is normally a mixture from one carpet, so the colours work in well together in good proportions. Where there is a choice of lengths the longer strands are better value.

However, some firms sell broken hanks, and 1 kg (2 lb) of olive green could consist of four hanks of different shades which tone with each other. This can be very useful when a variety of the same colour is needed for motifs or a shaded background. Wool can sometimes be bought cheaply in end-of-range colours. None of these methods of buying wool allows for repeats of the same colour. Therefore enough should be bought initially to complete a rug.

The most expensive way of buying wool is in hanks from stock. These colours can usually be bought in 225 g (8 oz) quantities and may be reordered. They are worth getting if the main design uses some of the cheaper ranges but smallish amounts of special colours are needed.

If you wish to order a particular shade by post, it is a great help to the firm if you send a piece of wool, material, wallpaper or some other specimen of the required shade.

its crispness with handling, whereas linen canvas keeps its original character and is very pleasant to work on. A size 18 needle with single wool is best used on this grade of canvas, which lends itself to more elaborate designs than the 5s or 4s.

Excellent rugs can be made on these three grades which are the most generally useful, but finer linen canvas is also available and can make a wonderful rug when used with the finer wool. The consideration here is time. On 5s canvas there are 25 knots per 2·5 cm^2 (1 sq in), on 8s there are 64, and on 10s there are 100. It would probably not be

Double thread canvases are available in a variety of widths and grades. The difference can be clearly distinguished between the coarse 4s canvas, the medium grade 5s and the very fine 8s.

worth spending so much effort on anything smaller than a 69 x 115 cm (27 x 45 in) rug, when it might take two hours to work one pile row. This is not intended to put off a keen rugmaker, but is a warning that it is a major undertaking to be approached after experience on coarser canvases. There is a great deal of scope for design on the finer canvases and the results can be exquisite.

Colour descriptions are not very useful in trying to obtain a good match.

Not all firms sell in the same way and it is always worth enquiring from a carpet factory how they sell their wools. Some sell only thrums but if the mixture consists of an interesting range of colours the resultant rug can be most successful.

Although accuracy in assessing the amount of wool required is difficult since so much depends on the individual worker, the following rough guide to quantities may be helpful: 5s canvas, short pile or flat stitches, 225 g (8 oz) per 31 cm^2 (1 sq ft). 8s canvas, short pile or flat stitches, 175 g (6 oz) per 31 cm^2 (1 sq ft).

Constantly threading needles is a tiresome task, so it is a good plan to have as many in use as the number of shades being used.

The length of wool in the needle should be restricted to 80-90 cm (32-36 in). Longer threads are awkward to control and unnecessary.

Brussels thrums is a much finer wool and comes in a double strand which should be untwisted and two or more strands used in the needle, depending on the canvas.

Hems and edges

When making a pile rug or one in flat stitches, the way of dealing with the hems and edges is slightly different, so it is better to consider each separately.

Pile rugs

The cut ends of the canvas must be dealt with first to prevent fraying. The far end can be oversewn roughly and left until the rug is nearly finished, when the exact number of rows still needed can be easily counted.

At the end where the rug is started, the canvas should be folded over about 5 cm (2 in) for 5s canvas and slightly less for finer ones. A double bar of the canvas must lie along the fold and all the holes in the two layers must lie exactly over one another since the work at the ends is done through the double thickness. Turn the raw edge upwards so that the pile will then hide the cut ends of the canvas.

The raw edge should be neatly and strongly oversewn to the canvas below, ensuring that the threads lie parallel. Use a cotton of the same colour as the canvas, otherwise the cotton may show on the underside. Finishing off the cotton satisfactorily along the raw edge can be tricky. Use the cotton double by threading the needle and knotting the ends together. When the thread is nearly used, cut it at the needle and tie the two short ends together through the knot of the new length of cotton. Cut off short.

The different effects of pile and flat stitches are shown in contrast in this blue rug, which is worked in both methods.

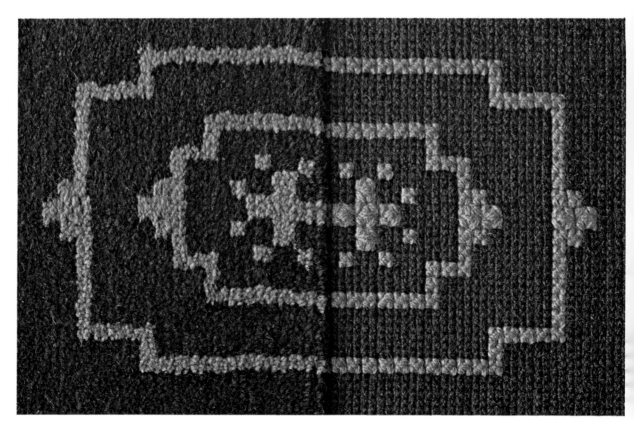

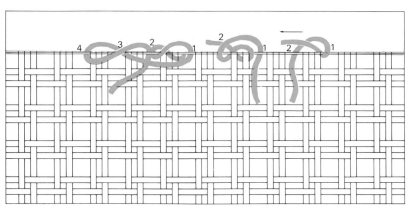

1 *Plaited edging stitch worked from right to left*

Flat stitch rugs

The cut end of the canvas is turned under and secured exactly as for pile rugs. The far end will most probably also have to be turned in at this stage since the work on a flat rug does not progress steadily from one end to the other like a pile rug. In making a flat rug the design may be outlined, the border completed, or the stitching done in any convenient sequence. This involves a very careful counting of the weft bars. For simplicity, count every 20 rows and run in a coloured thread. The sections can be checked easily and the total number worked out when turning the hem at the far end.

Remember to allow the right number of bars for the pattern plus the amount of canvas used by the edging plait. Fold, and allow the same depth of hem as at the beginning. Double check before cutting off.

It is a help when doing the edging plait if the corners of the canvas have already been very narrowly oversewn with a single strand of the wool to match the plait. Oversew about 1 cm ($\frac{1}{2}$ in) of the selvedge up to the corner, cover the point well, and do the same distance along the folded edge. The ends can be cut off short because the plait will be worked over it.

Occasionally, on 5s canvas particularly, little spikes of canvas tend to poke through the edging plait. To avoid this, continue the over-sewing along the folded edge over the top bar only, between each individual thread of the canvas. It is difficult to get a needle through the double selvedge and it may be better to use a finer needle for this. As 5s canvas is the grade recommended for a beginner in rug-making, the following instructions assume that this will be used. If the canvas is finer or coarser the numbers of lengths of wool are different, but the methods do not vary.

Working the plait

This stitch can be used for edging all needlemade rugs since it is hardwearing, simple to work and is easy to repair if the edges become worn. The edging plait may be started before the pile is begun on a pile rug, but in the case of a flat-stitch rug it should be worked after the rug is finished and stretched (figure 1).

Ideally, the plait down the selvedges should look the same width as that across the ends of the rug. Occasionally the canvas has an extra wide selvedge. If this is the case it can be turned in to reduce the width and the plait worked over the double thickness. Turn it to the same side as the turnover of the cut ends. If this results in very clumsy corners, a piece of the underneath selvedge may be cut away where it pokes out between the layers. This must be done carefully and not right up to the corners.

Pile rugs

With the cut edge of the canvas uppermost, the needle with two lengths of wool is:

1 brought up through the last hole on the right if making a very narrow edge, or (more usually) the next one down. Leave 5 cm (2 in) of wool lying at the back to be covered as the work progresses;

2 worked always from the back to the front so that the wool wraps over edge, the needle is brought up in the next hole to the left;

3 the needle is taken back through the original hole (from the back) so forming a single cross stitch over the top of the canvas;

4 the needle is taken forward three holes (to the fourth from the start);

5 the needle is then taken back two holes.

Repeat 4 and 5 (forward 3, back 2) until 'forward 3' comes out at the last hole in the line. Then, to reduce the length of the stitch, follow it by 'back 2, forward 2, back 1, forward 1' so that the end stitch is again a single cross.

From this end hole oversew the corner carefully and firmly. The narrow oversewing underneath will now help the top stitches to stay in place and not slip off the point. The canvas should be completely covered.

Begin the plait down the selvedge in exactly the same way as at the top. There is no need to complete the plait at this stage, so work only a little way down the selvedge. Return to the original corner and oversew round it, then start the plait down that selvedge. The only difference in the instructions is that 2 should read 'the needle is brought up in the next hole to the *right*'.

Always work from the back to the front so that the wool wraps over the edge of the canvas. If the covering seems thin, try an extra thread of wool in the needle. A turn of the needle every few stitches when working will ensure that the threads lie parallel, giving greater covering power and a neater finish.

A tiny pile rug worked in Surrey stitch.

When coming to the end of a thread, bring the needle up on a 'forward 3' and lay the end of the wool along the canvas, to be covered by subsequent stitches. The new thread should be run in the back of the plait and the needle brought out in the same hole, the next stitch being '2 back', so keeping the correct sequence of stitches.

Work a single line of long-legged cross stitch on the bar of canvas just inside the plait both along the end and down the sides. This will help to keep the pile from becoming worn at the edges. As pile rugs usually need no straightening when finished, the edging plait and the line of long-legged cross stitch can be worked across the end and then down the selvedges a few inches at a time, keeping just ahead of the rows of pile. There is no need to do it all at the beginning. If there is any doubt about whether the rug will need stretching, work the long-legged line but leave the plait until

after the rug is completed.

Flat stitch rugs

The line of long-legged cross stitch is omitted and the plait is worked after the rug is finished and stretched. Stretching involves nailing down and dampening. The working of the plait hides the nail holes.

Stitches

Rugs made with a needle may have a smooth surface or one with a pile. There are stitches to choose from for both finishes. Some people like the

look and feel of pile so much that they are prepared to accept the discipline of working row by row up the length of the rug. One advantage of this approach is that when the end is reached the rug is finished, whereas with a flat stitch rug all the interesting bits can be done first but then you are left with the duller parts and the background to finish. This is when energy tends to flag, so perhaps this method requires more determination.

The same wool worked in pile and a flat stitch has a different appearance. With the flat stitches it looks as it does in the hand, but in making a pile rug you can see the cut ends of the wool and the colours look much richer and deeper.

Short pile

Pile rugs are begun just inside the edging plait and the single line of long-legged cross stitch, with the length of canvas stretching away from the worker. The knots are worked across the width of the canvas one row at a time.

There is a choice of two knots for making the pile, Surrey stitch or Turkey knot. The latter produces a knot which exactly resembles that worked on a loom.

The two methods of achieving the pile look identical on the surface but are quite different on the back. On the whole the Surrey stitch is the more flexible in use. In Turkey knot only one thread of the double bar is picked up in each movement, whereas in Surrey stitch both threads are picked up. When using a large needle with four lengths of wool on a coarse canvas, or when using a finer canvas where the threads are closer together it is easier to work from one hole to the next rather than to attempt to work between the threads of each bar.

Surrey stitch

Each knot is made with two movements of the needle, the first being 'north to south' towards the worker, and the second 'east to west' from right to left, the needle coming out on the second movement at the hole where it first went in. In the figures the holes in the canvas are lettered so that the instructions are clear.

First movement (figures 2, 3). Insert the needle under a double weft bar of the canvas towards the worker from hole A to B. Pull the wool through until only about 1·5 cm ($\frac{3}{4}$ in) remains. The needle is taken away to the left and the short end doubled down, and the left thumb placed on it to keep it firm.

Second movement (figures 4, 5). With the length of wool flipped above the stitch being made, insert the needle at hole C and bring it out at hole A where the stitch began, so picking up a double warp bar. The needle passes over the loose length of wool. Draw the needle down firmly, and a knot is formed.

If only one stitch of the colour is needed, cut the wool off at the length of the pile, say 1·5 cm ($\frac{3}{4}$ in). If further stitches of the same colour are planned, put the left thumb on to the just-pulled length of wool to hold it in place and pass the needle under the weft bar of canvas from C to D. Because the wool from the previous stitch is being held down, the needle will go over the loop which is being made. Draw the needle through until the loop is the length of the required pile, move the left thumb to hold that down also, then carry the wool upwards as before and complete by making the 'east to west' stitch and pull the wool down to make a firm knot.

Each time the colour of the wool is to be changed, cut the wool at the length of the pile and begin the next stitch at A and B. Actually, when the loop is cut, the resultant pile will become marginally longer so allow a tiny bit extra so that the pile length matches up.

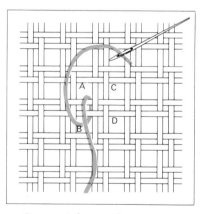

2 Surrey stitch, first step

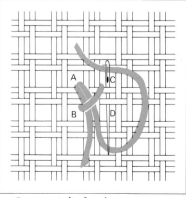

3 Surrey stitch, second step

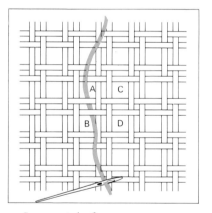

4 Surrey stitch, third step

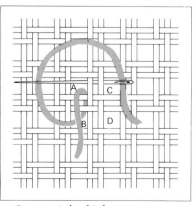

5 Surrey stitch, fourth step

For the next and following rows, insert the needle under the weft bar of canvas immediately above the last finished row (E to A).

Two lengths of 2-ply Axminster are needed on 5s canvas and probably a pile length of less than 1·5 cm ($\frac{3}{4}$ in) will be preferred. This can be adjusted with practice.

Turkey knot

This stitch is worked over the two threads of a double warp bar of the canvas. The warp bars only are used and the weft bars left bare.

Insert the needle between the threads of a bar, under the left-hand one, bringing it out in the adjacent hole. Draw the wool through and hold down the short end with the thumb as in Surrey stitch.

Flip the wool upwards as before and pick up the right-hand thread of the same bar, bringing the needle up between the two and pulling the

knot tight (figure 6). Cut off at the pile length if only one stitch of the colour is wanted. If further stitches in the same colour are to be worked, slip the just-pulled length of wool under the thumb as in Surrey stitch and work the next stitch over the adjacent bar to the right, and so on, leaving loops between the knots as before. The following row is worked above the weft bar just over the knots.

For both methods of working the pile, the line of loops may be cut every time a fresh needle is taken, or left until a row is completed and then cut. The easiest way to cut the pile is to insert the point of a pair of small sharp scissors into the loop, pull up until the loop is extended and then snip. This ensures that the loop is cut exactly in the middle, which helps to keep the pile even.

The length of loop will vary with the canvas used—about 1·5 cm

($\frac{3}{4}$ in) for 5s canvas and about 1 cm ($\frac{1}{2}$ in) for 8s is a good guide. It is wasteful to make the loops too long and have to trim them down, but it is better to err on that side to begin with than to make them too short, which will result in a motheaten appearance.

The pile will need to be scrabbled towards the worker to remove loose fluff. This can easily be done with the fingernails, or alternatively wear a rubber glove and stroke the pile hard with your fingers.

After the first 10 cm (4 in), the completed length of rug will be too thick to hold comfortably in the hand, so fold the worked canvas under so that only about 3 cm ($1\frac{1}{2}$ in) of the pile is still visible. Slip a long envelope into the fold. This will prevent the lower layer from being caught into the upper one when making the stitches. Cardboard, even thin, is not sufficiently flexible but some people have found a length of soft leather is ideal.

As the canvas is quite scratchy, it is sensible to wear an apron to protect clothes and stockings until the work part is long enough to cover the knees. Alternatively, sit at a table with the line being worked along the straight edge so that the canvas presents itself to the needle, and the finished part hangs downwards out of the way. Make sure that the table will survive needle scratches. Either way will achieve good results. The first way is preferable.

Flat stitches

These are started just inside the edging plait but with the unworked length of canvas facing towards the worker and the cut edge of the hem turned under and oversewn in the same way as for pile rugs.

When making pile rugs there is no reason to turn the canvas round. When working flat stitches this temptation does arise and must be resisted since it is almost bound to lead to trouble. It is very tiresome to have to unpick when mistakes

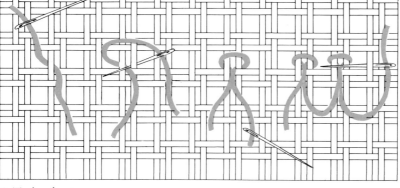

6 *Turkey knot*

7 *Cross stitch working in different directions*

have been made and it can be extremely difficult.

The group of stitches based on the cross stitch and its variations is excellent for smooth faced rugs and they combine well. In pile rugs all the ends of the wool are on the surface of the work, but with flat stitches they have to be finished underneath and this should be done neatly. If possible, run the ends into their own colour on the back. They show even less if they run on the straight of the canvas rather than diagonally.

Cross stitch

This is made by two stitches which slope across an intersection of the canvas at right angles to each other and can be worked easily in different directions. It is usually more satisfactory to complete each stitch before going on to the next, rather than to do a line of the underneath stitch and then come back afterwards to complete.

It is very important that the canvas is completely covered, so if the threads look rather sparse and an extra length of wool in the needle is too thick, lay a single strand of wool over the bar of canvas and work the stitches over this. The top half of the stitch must always lie in the same direction (bottom left to top right) and care should be taken to keep the threads in the needle lying parallel and not twisted (figure 7).

Long-legged cross stitch

This is very similar to the edging plait, but is worked on the flat, going forward 2, back 1, instead of 3 and 2 respectively. This can be done in straight lines backwards and forwards or up and down. It is the direction of the stitch which is turned, not the canvas.

If so desired this stitch may be used to work over the double canvas at the ends of a pile rug, starting the pile rows where the canvas becomes single. In this case the hem should be turned under because the pile will not hide the raw edge.

It is easier to work this stitch in lines of reasonable length rather than two or three stitches only. It is then very quick to do. Like the edging plait, it is begun with a single cross stitch and the first half is worked in the direction in which the plait is to travel. The stitches on the back of the work, except occasionally when changing direction, always lie in the opposite direction to the line of travel. That is to say, if the stitch is being worked across the canvas, those at the back are all vertical and vice versa. Figure 8 shows the stitch in both directions.

The reversed canvas shows the outline of patterns worked in Turkey knot.

As well as starting with a single cross, a line is ended in the same way, so 'forward 2, back 1' is followed by 'forward 1'. Where the pattern indicates a change of colour, the start and finish would be made like this. If simply ending a thread and starting a fresh one, go down on 'forward 2' and run the end forwards under the bar being worked

over. It can be brought up and down again once to hold it in position. Run the new thread through the backs of the stitches just worked and bring the needle out in the hole where it would have emerged had the stitch with the old thread been completed. Then work 'back 1' so that the sequence of stitches is maintained.

If a pattern is being worked in long-legged cross stitch and a single cross is required in the design, an ordinary cross stitch seems rather thin in comparison. To increase the weight of the cross stitch, work the lower half twice and work a single stitch on the top as usual. When working single crosses, the top stitch should lie in the same direction throughout the rug. Do not alter it to go with the direction of the plait.

Long-legged cross stitch is quite the most useful of all the flat stitches in the group, but the others provide good contrasts and changes of texture and can be used in various combinations to great effect.

Deep long-legged cross stitch

This is constructed in exactly the same way as the previous stitch, working 'forward 2, back 1' but over two bars of the canvas instead of one, so doubling only the width of a row of stitches. It makes an excellent divider when worked down the length of a rug, and two rows with a band of rice stitch in between, using different colours, make a good border (figure 9).

Rice stitch

This makes a nice 'nubbly' texture and contrasts well with the even ribbed effect of the long-legged cross stitch. The foundation is a large cross made over two bars of the canvas each way, and then each corner is crossed by a small diagonal stitch (figure 10). The stitches at the back should be straight up or across the canvas which makes a neat back and a better looking stitch on the front, too. If the stitches at the back are diagonal, those on the front have a flat look which detracts from their appearance (figure 11).

The small blue rug is worked in two flat stitches, and the changes of texture created by this subtle combination are quite visible.

Where several rows of rice stitch are worked together the canvas may

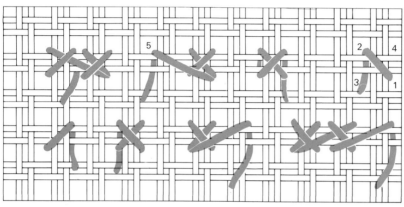

8 Long-legged cross stitch working right to left (above) and left to right (below)

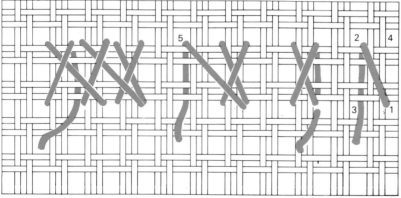

9 Deep long-legged cross stitch working right to left

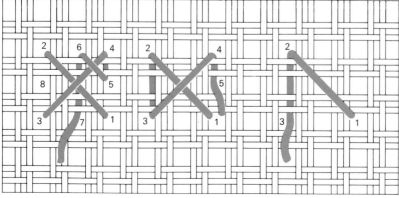

10 Rice stitch, first three steps

be inclined to show. If so, a row of back stitches should be worked between them.

Back stitch

This can be worked along any line of holes in the canvas, both straight across or down, and diagonally. It is used for covering the canvas between or beside a variety of stitches.

If working between two rows of rice stitch, bring the needle up through the second hole in the line and down through the first, then up through the third and down through the second and so on, making a series of short stitches on the surface and longer ones behind.

Rice stitch may need this as the wool pulls slightly towards the centre of each stitch, tending to bare the canvas; if rice stitch is used between lines of ordinary or long-legged cross stitch the back stitching would not be necessary.

Where a flat stitch rug has an odd number of bars in the width, and therefore has a centre stitch, it is often convenient to have available a big stitch worked over three bars.

Double cross rice stitch

This stitch fills this need and consists of a large cross worked diagonally over three bars in each direction, and over this a straight cross, where in order to be central, the needle does not go into a hole, but splits the double bars of the canvas. Small diagonal crosses are made across the corners, using the same split holes for the needle as the straight cross uses (figures 12, 13).

It is rather extravagant in wool, like the rice stitch itself, and it stands out above most other stitches so may show signs of wear before them. For this reason it might be as well to work it after the surrounding canvas has been covered so that the stitches and the finishing-off of ends are not sewn-in by other stitches and can easily be unpicked and worked again. However, the rug should take a lot of wear before it becomes necessary to do this.

An example of the use of this stitch is in the blue and green rug illustrated, where it is worked in all the large crosses down the centre of the smooth end. Note that the top stitch of the cross for both rice and double cross rice should run in the same direction throughout.

When working with rice or double cross rice stitch on a line of pattern which does not divide exactly into two or three as the case may be, one or two stitches must be worked to fill the gap. Long-legged or cross stitch may be used, placed centrally or at the ends of the line.

Soumak

This is another flat stitch and when it is worked on canvas it looks

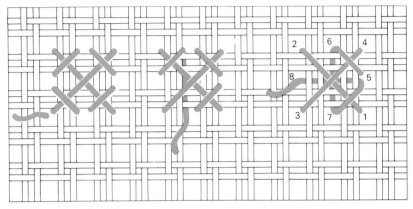

11 Rice stitch, final three steps

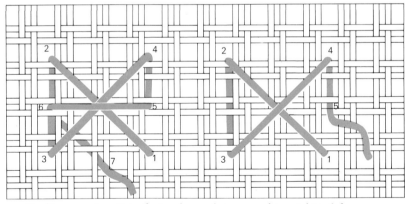

12 Double-cross rice stitch, first and second steps, working right to left

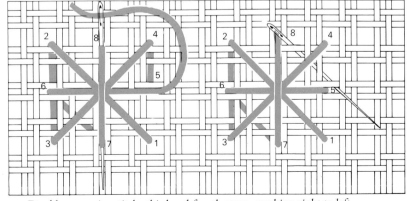

13 Double-cross rice stitch, third and fourth steps, working right to left

exactly like the same stitch done on a loom. In appearance it resembles stocking stitch in knitting. The stitches are closely interlocked and have a very smooth finish which helps the wearing qualities of the rugs. This stitch is attractive and unusual and is fascinating to do. The working of the stitch is quite different from all the others used in that the canvas is held with the selvedges running across the knees and each stitch makes a V whose point faces the worker.

The stitch is begun by bringing the needle up between two threads of a weft double bar in the canvas (not where the bars cross each other). The needle is taken up over two warp bars and picks up both threads of the bar which was split, and returns to the original hole, making a V (figures 14-17).

If working downwards, the needle comes up between the threads of the next double bar below and the stitch is repeated. It can also be worked diagonally or sideways, so the outlining of a pattern can be done and filled in later, or a border finished first.

The top one of a line of stitches is worked over two double bars and each subsequent stitch uses one fresh bar and one from the previous stitch, so when making a chart for a rug in Soumak stitch it must have one fewer squares than the number of warp bars in the width of the canvas, 108 on paper for 109 bars of canvas.

To work in Soumak stitch a design made for other flat stitches or for pile, one extra bar may be gained by making the two inner threads of canvas on one selvedge serve as a bar. As this will reduce the width of the selvedge on that side the one on the other side will probably have to be folded to make them an equal width.

It is very important to be accurate in following the pattern as the stitches are so closely interlocked that it is difficult to unpick mistakes. Perhaps the most satisfactory way of

A small rug derived from the Dagestan rug (right) worked in Soumak, giving a smooth, hard-wearing finish.

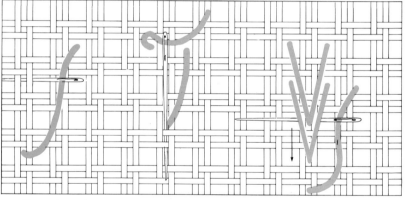

14 Soumak stitch

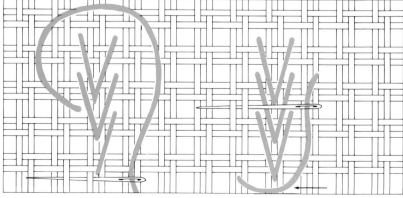

15 Soumak stitch worked in different directions

108

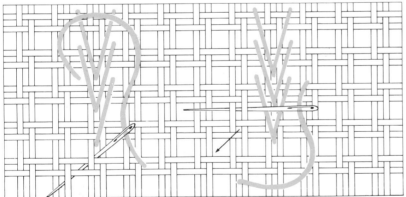

16 *Soumak stitch worked in different directions*

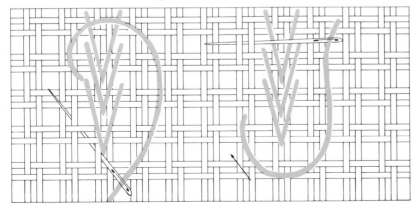

17 *Soumak stitch worked in different directions*

ensuring accuracy before much interlocking occurs is first to complete the outlining of borders and main motifs, so that you can be certain these are correctly placed in relation to each other. Once the main structure of the design has been established the later filling-in is much less likely to be wrong. Practise this first on a sample piece, since it is easy to miss occasional stitches when filling in.

The stitch needs care in regard to tension because, if the wool is pulled too tightly, the rug may acquire a waist which is difficult to straighten. Only use enough tension to pull the wool through the canvas, and the wool in the eye of the needle should pass easily through the split bars.

The 2-ply used singly may be thick enough to cover the 5s canvas, but two threads are usually too thick. Brussels thrums used in as many threads as are found satisfactory may be used, or possibly one thread of 2-ply with one of Brussels thrums in a matching shade to produce the right thickness.

Soumak is a fascinating stitch to work and shows to its best advantage when used on its own.

The little Soumak ruglet was worked in Brussels thrums on 8s canvas. The design comes from a detail in an old Kuba Dagestan rug. The octagons were placed in pairs on the field with smaller patterns between. The yellow background has small circles and crosses in a darker shade and although they are only just visible, they relieve the otherwise rather flat effect. The ribbon edging comes from the same source and makes a particularly pretty border design. To ensure that the colours match at the corners, there are adjoining yellows in the centre of each side and end, instead of alternate pink and yellow all the way round.

Not all embroidery stitches are suitable for rugmaking, but a book like *Dictionary of Embroidery Stitches* by Mary Thomas is worth looking through for alternatives to those suggested here. The choice should lie among those with hardwearing qualities, such as those which interlock, are tied down, and/or slope across the canvas. Nothing with a loose thread across the surface should be considered, and you should bear in mind that the stitches must hide the canvas completely. Tent stitch and French stitch would both be suitable.

Left-handed workers should follow the instructions for the edging plate and both the long-legged cross stitches, but the working of all the other stitches should be reversed (use a mirror on the diagrams) and the pile stitches worked from right to left along the rose.

Finishing flat-stitch rugs

It is not usually necessary to finish a pile rug in any way except to trim off any unevenness with a pair of sharp scissors, blades 10 cm (4 in) long or more. If this seems difficult on the flat, the rug can be eased over the straight edge of a table so that each row can be seen and trimmed individually.

The appearance of flat stitch rugs is greatly improved if they are dampened and stretched, using a clean wood floor or similar surface rather larger than the size of the rug.
1 With the rug facing upwards, tack one long side about 2·5 cm (1 in) away from the line of a floorboard or along a ruled line. Stretch only enough to make it lie flat. The tacks should be about 5 cm (2 in) apart and if small brass nails are used there will be no risk of rust marks.
2 One of the ends must be tacked so that it is held at right angles to the long side.
3 Fix the second end so that it also lies at right angles to the long side, and equals the first end in length. Tack the other long side. Your fingers may not be strong enough to pull the rug into shape, and a pair of long-nosed pliers is a great help. They grip the edge of the work and

are thin enough for the tacks to be hammered down quite close by.
4 So that there are no scallops which will show afterwards, put in extra tacks so that all are about 2·5 cm (1 in) apart.
5 Take a sponge and a basin of cold water. Press the well-wetted sponge all over the surface of the rug, using sufficient water for the canvas to be moist, not simply the wool. It is surprising how much is needed, do not be too timid to use sufficient.
6 Cover the rug with a towel or old blanket. If ordinary tacks have been used, cover them with strips of brown paper to avoid rust marks. Leave the rug for a week or more to become absolutely dry.
7 Remove the tacks and work the edging plait. If a pile rug needs straightening, it should be stretched face downwards so that the moisture can reach the canvas.

Rya rugs

The Rya rugs from Scandinavia have long, shaggy pile with many weft threads between each line of knots. A Rya-type rug can be made quite successfully on a 4s canvas foundation. As four threads of wool are used in the needle some very subtle colour effects can be achieved.

Two or three rows of deep long-legged cross stitch between the rows of knots has the same effect of separating the pile rows as the many weft threads on the woven rugs. They are practically invisible when the rug is finished. A great many uninteresting colours can be used up working these flat stitch rows, but the colours should not make too sharp a contrast with the pile or they may be just visible through it and spoil the appearance. Three threads are used in the needle for the flat stitch background and for the edging plait unless the wool happens to be a little thicker than usual, when two may be enough to cover the canvas.

The colours in the rugs may be brilliant and exciting or very simple, and as a rule all blending into one

another. With four threads of wool in mixed shades in the needle, very gradual changes of colour are possible as the work progresses.

Blocks of colour merging into neighbouring blocks, and simple abstract designs or big geometric forms are usually more typical and successful than anything in the way of a precise pattern. There are fascinating opportunities of experimenting as the pile is so long that the knot can be pulled out and the wool used again. Shapes and colours may be tried out and altered easily if not quite right.

Method of working
Fold and stitch the hems in the usual way, turning the cut edge under, and start by oversewing the corners and working the edging plait across the

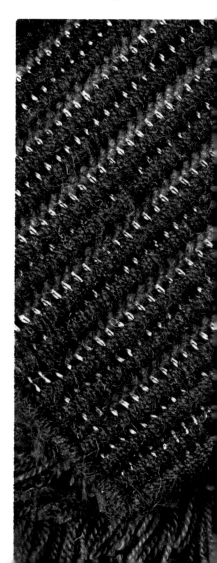

end. Then work three rows of deep long cross stitch in alternate directions if a 5 cm (2 in) pile is wanted, or four rows for 6 cm (2½ in) pile.

If the pile stitches are worked right up to the selvedges across the rows, the pile itself will hang over the edges, so it is advisable to work three stitches (covering four holes of the canvas) of ordinary long-legged cross stitch at each end of every pile row, using two threads only. Then work the first row of knots, and when the loops are cut the pile should reach to the edge of the rug, including the edging plait.

Work two rows of deep long-legged cross stitch for a 5 cm (2 in) pile, or three rows for a 6 cm (2½ in) pile. Then work the second row of knots, remembering the three stitches of ordinary long-

legged cross stitch at each end. The subsequent rows of pile, when cut, should overlap the preceding row by half its length.

After the final row of knots, work one line of deep or ordinary long-legged cross stitch and then the edging plait. The edging plait on the selvedges may be worked before or after the rest of the rug.

Some people like to work all the flat background before starting the pile, in which case the unworked length of canvas faces towards the worker as for the other flat stitches. This saves a good deal of turning of the rug, as when working the pile the unworked canvas, as usual, faces away from the worker.

The pile may be worked in Turkey knot or Surrey stitch, but the latter is rather easier when using

a large needle with four threads of wool.

When making a chart for a Rya rug it is only necessary to show the pile rows, omitting all the flat-stitch rows. This results in a very squashed-looking chart, since the width is correct but, for a 1·25 m (4 ft) rug, the length is reduced to about 23 cm (9 in).

It is simpler to sketch the general idea on a rug-sized sheet of paper and then to transfer the outlines on to the canvas by running a thread round, as suggested for the exploded cut paper method of designing.

Colour and design

The basic requirements for making any rugs are a good light, canvas, wool, needles, a pair of small sharp scissors plus a larger pair for trimming the pile, and usually a pattern to work from.

For several reasons it is more practical for a rug to be rectangular in shape rather than to have curved sides. To begin with, the canvas is bought by the metre and it is wasteful to cut pieces off unnecessarily. The edging plait is worked most easily on the straight of the canvas, both up the selvedges and across the turned-in hem when it is worked through the double canvas (like the stitches of the rug itself). On a curve, no two holes lie exactly over each other and it is much harder to achieve a neat finish. If a rectangular rug becomes worn unevenly it can be turned round, which a half-moon cannot.

Many books are available about oriental rugs. Many have excellent coloured plates which provide ideas for designs and help in planning the balance of colours which some people find difficult.

Whenever the opportunity occurs

The Rya rug from Scandinavia is easily recognized by its long, shaggy pile. Magnificent splashes of colour can be used to great effect when designing a Rya. (Designed and worked by Mrs Joan Droop.)

look at oriental rugs, old and modern, and also look with a critical eye at all sorts of textiles. Try to analyse what is pleasing in the way of colour, proportion and balance, so that it becomes easier to imagine how colours will look together when planning a rug.

Choice of colour

The choice of colour is a very personal thing and in making rugs at home and planning the design yourself, the setting and even the personality of the user can be taken into consideration. In time the original colours will become less vivid. Turn to the back of old rugs and it will be apparent how much fading has occurred over the years. Modern dyes may fade rather less than the old dyes but some fading is probably inevitable. Ordinary wear will also dim the colours to some extent. All this must be taken into account when planning a rug.

Even the most complicated of designs is more effective if restricted to four or five colours, although there may well be several shades of each for variety. Several shades of just one colour can be very effective.

On the whole, a dark shade of any of the colours being used is better than black for edges and dividers (lines between different borders and between the borders and the field) and a cream or stone shade is more pleasing than white, which tends to stand out too much.

Colour sense is something which can be developed and it is helpful to make a note of pleasing colour combinations and proportions. A batch of thrums will consist of colours which go together and it is often useful to get some extra wool in one of the darker shades to use for edges and dividers.

A good balance can be achieved by the judicious use of complementary colours. A rug in cool colours, blues and greens, could have touches of warm colours, oranges and/or reds. Similarly, a rug in warm colours benefits from the addition of some cool colours. It is essential to have correct amounts of each, so the additions have to be planned with discretion.

A soft green background with darker green for edges and dividers will allow many brighter colours to be used in the pattern. The link rug has an unexpected mixture of dark blue for all the edges, dividers and outlining, with shades of greens, pinks, reds, tan and creamy colours. Dark brown is a very useful colour for edges and outlines. Most lighter and brighter colours look well with it. The Turkey knot rug has a satisfactory combination of several greens, reds and oranges.

A rug will be seen on the floor and at a distance, so make sure the effect really is what you intended it to be. When the colours have been chosen provisionally leave them on the floor for a while in approximately the right proportions and change them if necessary until the right look is obtained. Something seen

---

A small blue flat stitch rug worked in geometric T-shapes.

and liked on your knee does not necessarily look well at a range of 3m (10 ft). As a rug will last for many years, it is worth spending time at this stage to make it as perfect as possible.

The same wool worked in flat stitches and in pile will look quite different. The contrasting pile rug shows how the colour deepens when only the cut ends of the wool are visible. Consequently it is rather less easy to be sure that the chosen colours will be right when planning a pile rug than a flat stitch rug. So it can be reassuring to work a sample piece about 30 cm (1 ft) wide on which a few combinations of colours can be tried out. It may only be a matter of checking that the chosen colours will look as you intended with their neighbours, but sometimes it is a decision about which green will look best, or whether a tan shade would be a better background for small motifs. Work the design with a 7-10 cm (3-4 in) width of each colour to see which you prefer, and if necessary a further piece of whatever comes next to it,

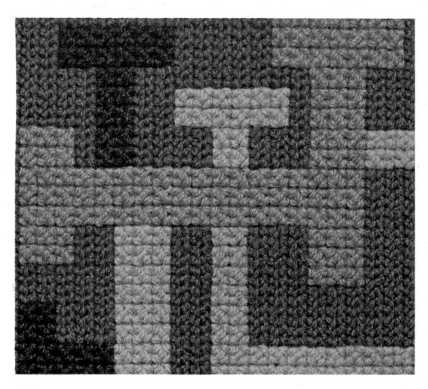

to make sure these colours tie in well.

If a mistake in colour has been made and a motif on a pile rug absolutely must come out, it is quite simple to unpick by lifting the tying-down part of the knot with the end of the needle. Avoid using scissors if you can in case you cut the canvas by mistake. The working of the fresh knots when there is pile all around is a very fiddly business. The best way of doing it is to use a sticky tape to hold the surrounding pile back out of the way. This tape peels off very easily without causing damage, so use plenty of it to ensure that no loose ends are sewn in.

A pile rug worked in Turkey knot.

Planning a design

In most crafts today it is possible to buy all the materials and the pattern complete in a kit, so no thought need be given to the design except for choosing from the selection available. The techniques of rugmaking are usually acquired quite quickly, but the idea of actually designing anything is unusual and alarming. But planning your own individual design can be so exciting and rewarding that it is well worth trying. People who at first imagine that they cannot do it, are often surprised at what they achieve.

Those who are able to draw freehand will soon learn what kind of design is best on the canvas and will be able to transfer these easily on to graph paper. Planning does not require this ability since the graph paper and the canvas are a discipline in themselves. Once the idea of making an outline and how to manage a curve are absorbed, it becomes possible to draw all sorts of things. Try to work out some shapes in pencil on graph paper. Start with stars, octagons and oval shapes. You will find that the outlining makes the shapes come alive. Then subdivide the area inside to make the design more interesting. On 5s canvas something fairly geometric is usually better than curves. The smallest possible circle on canvas is really an octagon over six squares. A real circle uses 13 which takes about 4 cm ($1\frac{1}{2}$ in) on 8s canvas and 7 cm ($2\frac{1}{2}$ in) on 5s. See how the circle is made to go round with a gradually shortening line of stitches in one direction, then one or more diagonally before the same series of stitches running at right angles. The outlining is done on the inside of the circle and may leave one or more stitches in between (figure 20).

If this seems too difficult to begin with, try copying on to graph paper some of the ideas in this book and putting together an individual design. This will give you practice in fitting the patterns into the space

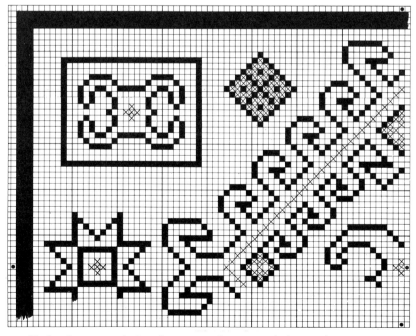

18 *Turkey knot rug—$\frac{1}{4}$-size chart on graph paper with dots marking centre of stitches*

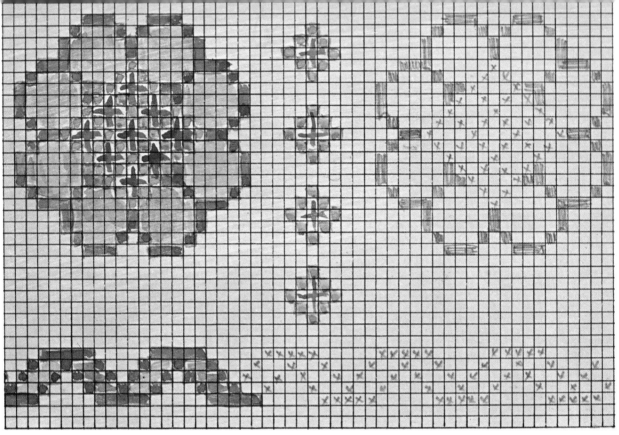

19 *Various designs and colours planned on graph paper*

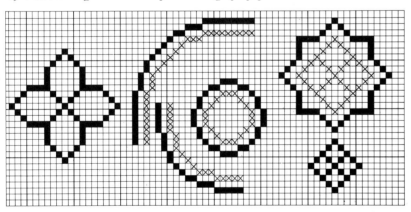

20 *Shapes planned on graph paper – (a) star made up of four hexagonal shapes (b) curves and circles – (c) diamond star – (d) small diamond*

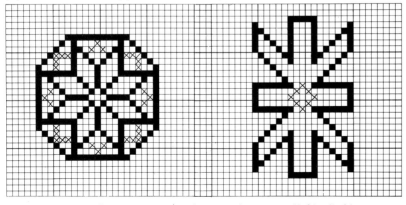

21 *Octagonal motif incorporating star design within a cross (left); double cross motif (right)*

and making neat corners.

A rug need not have a complicated pattern. Something quite simple may be preferred, perhaps zigzags or stripes with an edging of one of the darker colours as a frame. Or the colours in a batch of mixed thrums may be sorted out, placed on a length of canvas on the floor and arranged and rearranged until the heaps and squiggles of the different shades make a pleasing effect. Then run a thread of the appropriate colour round each shape so that the arrangement may be kept to while working. This is how the mixed thrums rug was made. It is an interesting way of arriving at an abstract design.

Cut paper methods

Another way of working out a design is to cut newspaper to the size of the proposed rug (or half the size if one large enough is not available). Fold it in half once each way. Then cut a jagged triangle from the folded corner. The holes in the canvas lie in straight and diagonal lines, so for simplicity in subsequent working cut the paper vertically, horizontally or diagon-

ally. Spread the paper out and there will be a jagged diamond in the centre. The cut-out pieces can be divided into four along the folds and the resulting triangles arranged in the corners of the paper. This is the basis of a design, and there are unlimited variations on the theme. If the sloping lines are not on the true diagonal they are slightly more difficult to transfer subsequently on to graph paper, but if the design is satisfactory in other respects, go ahead and draw the diagonals as cut and then square them (figure 22).

In another cut paper method, you can experiment with two rectangles of paper, one plain and one coloured. Measurements of the larger must be in the same proportions as the canvas. If the size of the rug is to be 56 x 84 cm (22 x 33 in) the proportion is 1 : 1½ so the paper could be 30 x 45 cm (12 x 18 in) or 25 x 37 cm (10 x 15 in) and the other piece rather smaller. Cut the smaller one into eight or ten irregular shapes and explode them on to the larger, keeping them in their proper relationship to each other so that if they are pushed together they will reform their original rectangle (figure 23).

If the smaller piece is cut more or less horizontally the effect will tend to be tranquil. If vertically, then it will be more exciting. One way to try out variations in the arrangement is to lay the larger piece on a cork mat and impale the cut bits on to the cork with pins, or you could use a ceiling tile in place of the cork.

An unlimited number of arrangements may be made, or rectangles cut up, until a satisfactory design is arrived at. Then a line should be drawn round each piece before it is removed. The design is now ready for enlarging and transferring to the canvas.

Enlarging a design

Following figure 24, mark the corners of the rectangle A B C D, and pin it securely to the top left-hand corner of a sheet of paper larger than the canvas. Rule in the diagonal line AC and extend it to the far corner of the paper at F.

In rugmaking, the width of the canvas is usually the measurement that cannot be altered, so rule BC and extend to G, making CG the width of the rug. Make sure that the angle at G is 90°. Rule a line from G to cut the diagonal CF, and mark this point H. Rule DC and extend across the paper to E, and with a right angle at H rule a line upwards to cut CE at J. All the corners must be right angles, and CG measure the same as JH, and CJ the same as GH.

The new rectangle will be the width of the proposed rug, and of the same proportions as the original design. Now rule lines each way across the centres of the original and the new pattern, and divide the sides of both into half and half again. Subdivide as necessary, so that the design can be transferred easily on to the larger paper by copying where the lines of the design cross the ruled lines on the original pattern.

More ambitious patterns may be based on designs used in old rugs. There are many available for study in museums and many more can be seen in country houses open to the

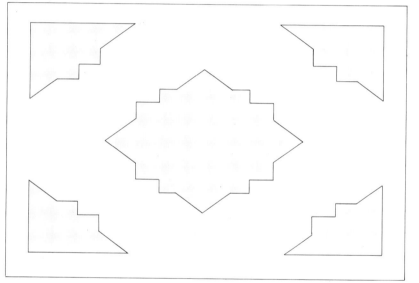

22, 23 Design using cut paper method

115

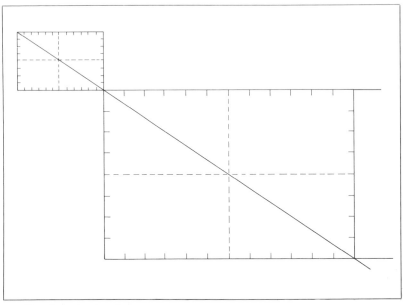

24 *Plan for enlarging designs*

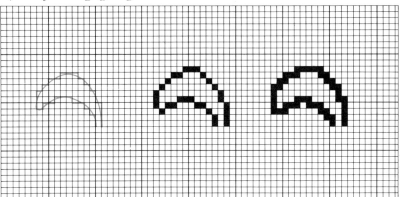

25 *Leaf design on graph paper showing squaring and correct (left) and incorrect (right) outlining*

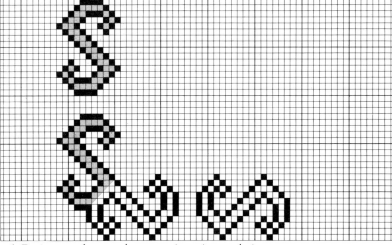

26 *Design traced on graph paper using mirror technique*

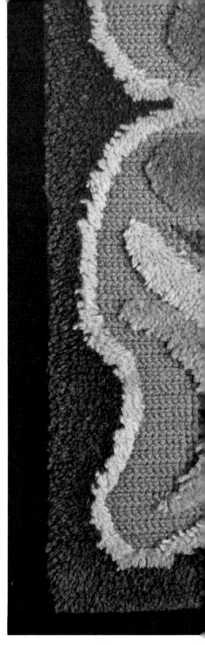

public. When looking at rugs, or at photographs or illustrations for ideas, a particular motif can be picked out. There is no need to think that the whole of any design must be used. Carry a pad of squared paper to jot down small patterns that appeal to you and which could contribute to a finished design. Turn to the back of a rug and the arrangement of knots can be seen quite easily.

You will notice that almost all the motifs on these rugs are outlined with a darker or contrasting shade. This emphasizes the patterns. A motif that is not outlined will tend to recede into the background of the design and possibly disappear.

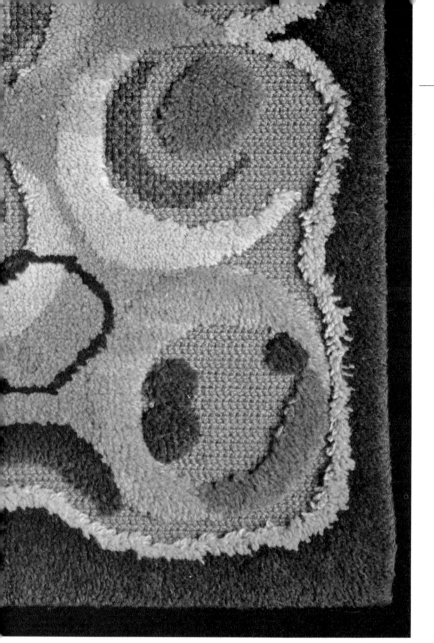

make better corners than others. Then copy the one you prefer on to graph paper (figure 26).

If the design on a rug is a cottage in a garden, or a cat sitting on a mat, it is difficult to hide an accidental stain in one corner by turning the rug. Although there is no need to have a symmetrical design it is usually more satisfactory in use if there is no one obvious right way.

When planning a rug for a child, the pattern might include animals or birds, or perhaps nice big letters round the edge. But remember that the years go by, so try to make something that will not seem too babyish later on.

Alternate stripes of pile and flat stitches could have different motifs on each. The flat lines need to be charted wider than they are to appear when the rug is finished to allow for the pile encroaching as it lies over. If the cut ends of the canvas come in a flat stitch section, turn the hem under.

Using graph paper

A detailed design should be worked out on graph paper which can be bought from most stationers. The most useful graph paper for rugmakers has eight or ten divisions per 2·5 cm (1 in).

The paper with eight per 2·5 cm (1 in) is excellent for planning a rug on 5s or 8s canvas. For 8s, the design will come out the right size, but for 5s it will be on a smaller scale, so the rug will work out larger than the pattern. If wishing to make the pattern the correct size for 5s canvas, use graph paper with ten divisions per 2·5 cm (1 in) when two small squares in each direction (four small squares in all) will be the exact equivalent to one knot or stitch.

Freehand designs

If a freehand design is to be out-lined, first square it. Replace the curved or sloping line as nearly as possible by a stepped line following the sides of the small squares on the graph paper. Remember that the outline stitches are those which have this line as their inside boundary.

On the chart this method is shown with a leaf drawn freehand and then squared, and finally outlined. If a design is already squared on to graph paper but not outlined, use the stepped line as the inside boundary for the outline stitches (figure 25).

Always keep your eyes open for ideas which can crop up in all sorts of unexpected places. It is worth cutting out and keeping illustrations of both old and modern rugs which turn up in Sunday supplements, advertisements and magazines. Put them into a folder with other jottings and they might provide inspiration at some future date.

Some cross stitch and Fair Isle patterns lend themselves to rug-making, and when planning borders these and many others have to be made to go neatly round corners. The best way to do this is to acquire a small rectangular mirror without a frame or bevelled edge. Place it diagonally across the design, and a reflection of a right-angled repeat will appear. Move the mirror to and fro as some parts of any pattern

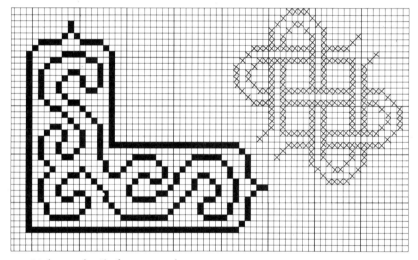

27 Link rug, detail of pattern and corner

(Left) The link rug, named for its intriguingly interlaced 'links' surrounded by a border of flowers. The inspiration for the motifs came from a much older rug (right) which is from the collection at the Victoria and Albert Museum, London.

These designs are mostly blocked in, but at the planning stage a cross on the paper is enough to indicate a stitch and is easier to rub out if adjustments have to be made.

In a symmetrical design it is only essential to work out half, or even a quarter, of the chart. But it is much easier for a beginner to appreciate the overall effect if the whole is charted. There will inevitably be a lot of rubbing-out to do before everything is exactly right, so use a soft pencil and a good rubber.

A border is not essential. Instead perhaps an edging of a darkish colour may be worked as a frame to the field. If a border is planned, about one-third of the total width is a good proportion to aim at. In a rug 56 cm (22 in) wide, this would work out at just over 18 cm (7 in), about 18 stitches down each side on 5s canvas. This would allow for one or two stripes, although a border on wider canvas could be divided into several.

It makes for a good appearance if the corners are symmetrical. But very frequently the planned pattern will not fit into the space, no matter how it is juggled. When this happens, and before abandoning the plan, begin by getting the corners right and work the design inwards. The centre will need an adjustment but this will obviously be intended, whereas poor corners will look like mistakes.

The opposite corners of the link rug match each other. But the design would have been better if there had been a flower in each corner and the meander, a winding motif into which flowers and leaves are fitted, adjusted in the centre of the sides and ends. This would not have been difficult to do to balance the design.

Link rug

The scheme for this rug originated from a photograph of an intertwining pattern in a sixteenth century carpet from the V and A Museum, London. A magnifying glass was used to clarify the details.

The design was planned for 8s canvas, 92 cm (36 in) wide and the link pattern in the field and the three border stripes were pencilled in. There were now quite large spaces to be filled in the field, and another photograph from the same collection yielded a suitable motif. This went into the centre. It was halved to fit along the sides and ends where it faced inwards. One point to note is that the red snake pattern in the central motif had to be lengthened where it was used at the sides, and drawn into a right angle at the corners (figure 27).

If the pattern on a border stripe has a series of flowers, diamonds or other small designs, whether joined or not, the length they take up can be varied considerably by leaving one stitch extra between some of them. If there are sometimes three instead of two stitches between motifs this will not be at all obvious so start by having one in each corner and experiment with the spaces between each, both across the end and up the length of the pattern.

Flower rug

Flowers in many forms appear in eastern rugs and two of them have been used in the design for the flower rug (as illustrated on the previous pages). The carnations in the border have been arranged so that there is one in each corner. Because they would not fit neatly otherwise, those in the end borders are wider apart than those down the sides and their stalks and leaves differ in order to fit into the space available. The centre block is an arrangement of the same flowers in the rectangle, and the tulips are typical of Ladik prayer rugs. Both motifs were charted from photographs using a magnifying glass (figure 28).

A particularly pleasant batch of thrums was used and although in theory only 2 kg (4½ lb) wool was necessary, 2·5 kg (6 lb) wool was bought to make sure of having enough of all the colours. An extra 0.5 kg (1 lb) wool to match the dark green was added, as the edges and dividers needed quite a lot of that colour.

Spider rug

The spider rug (illustrated on the opposite page) was enlarged from a medallion on the border of an Anatolian rug, and was worked mainly in long-legged cross stitch, with rice stitch and deep long-legged cross stitch, both of which make a change of texture. The Ss on the border are so bold that they need no outlining. They were extended on the corners so that they went round happily (figure 29). Some had one stitch less in their length to fit into the space, but this is not apparent except on a very close inspection. The background of the border used several darkish greens in haphazard blocks. Some of the inner background also had mixed shades, although these were deliberately shaded from darker on the outside edge to lighter further in. The centre background was all one colour.

When using a mixture of shades it is usually more satisfactory to have a definite plan to the shading, or even to have lines of each colour in turn giving an all-over effect, rather than to work individual stitches in different colours which only achieves speckles, although in pile rugs if two near shades are used together in the needle the effect is pleasant. Try out some shading of this sort to see how it looks.

If the required colours seem to be unobtainable it is possible to experiment with commercial dyes, probably blended to produce the right shades. Also many darkish and uninteresting wools can be dyed dark brown, producing a batch of related shades to use for edges and outlining. The same treatment could be given to lightish colours dyed a soft green. The batch finishes in shades of the same colour to make a very satisfactory shaded background.

Planning a pile rug

The planning for the diamond rug overleaf is fairly typical of the method for any design which has to be charted. The canvas chosen was 5s in a 56 cm (22 in) width which is a good one for a starter. At first it might take three-quarters of an hour to work a row of knots but speed comes with practice. This rug would probably take something under one hundred hours to finish. If the work is enjoyed it whets the appetite for a more ambitious project.

Unless making a rug to fit into a space with different proportions, the length is usually one and a half to one and three-quarter times the width, making this one 84-97 cm (33-38 in) long. For a first rug something quite simple may be preferred, but once a design has been charted the real work has been done. After that, however complicated the pattern, it is really only a matter of doing the stitches correctly and counting carefully to ensure each stage is accurate.

In all rug stitches, it is the bars, not the holes, which are important, and the 56 cm (22 in) canvas has 109 bars in the width.

Using a soft pencil, begin by ruling a line down one side of a sheet of 8s graph paper. Count 109 squares across the width and rule another line for the other edge of the work. Rule lines one square inside each of these for the line of

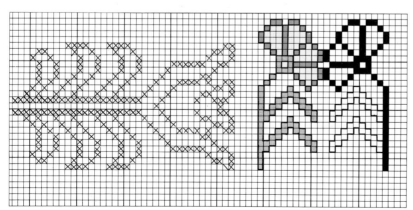

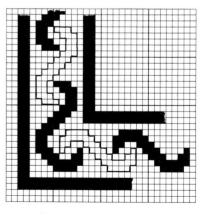

28 *Flower design (left) and carnation motif (right) planned on graph paper*

29 *S-shape arranged round corner*

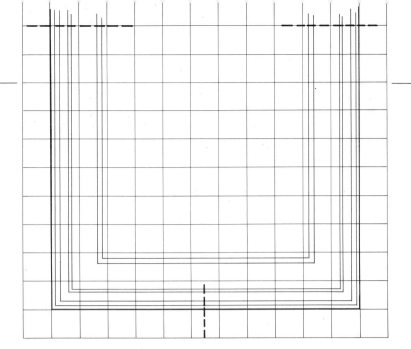

30 Border plan for pile rug

long-legged cross stitch just inside the plait. Rule two lines across the bottom between the two sides. If you prefer to work on 10s graph paper, two small squares each way equals one knot on the canvas (figure 30).

If a border is not wanted, a band of a darkish colour will make a frame for the field. If there is to be a border, about 17 to 20 stitches would be a reasonable width. The diamond rug was planned using the following stitches and colours:

2 rows of the darkish colour of the plait—2 stitches
3 rows of small slanting pattern—3 stitches
1 row divider—1 stitch
1 line of elongated diamonds—9 stitches
2 row divider—2 stitches

Including the single line of long-legged cross stitch, the border came to a total of 18 stitches on each side of the rug, reducing the width of the field to 73 stitches.

The elongated diamonds did not go neatly into the corners, so the two-stitch divider was extended to make small squares into which a different motif was fitted. The same diamond theme continued in the field of the rug. At this stage the centre stitch in the width was marked and also the approximate centre in the length of the rug.

One-quarter of the whole rug was fully plotted on the chart, so when working the rug, the second half of each row exactly mirrored the first. For the further end of the rug the pattern was turned round in order to work from the centre to the far end.

Some of the border diamonds had different spaces between them as they could not fit evenly into the

Inspiration for this spider rug (top) came from the border medallion of an Anatolian rug. It is worked in a variety of flat stitches. (Below) A Caucasian rug from which came the design for the Turkey knot rug.

available lengths. An adjustment was made in the middle of the lines of the slanting pattern so that the corners would match. The small diamonds in the field could have been arranged differently, or omitted altogether if preferred.

The total length of the rug as planned was 91 cm (36 in), so 1·1 m (1¼ yd) of canvas was bought to allow for the hems and any amendment of the design as the work progressed. The area was about 0·5 m² (5½ ft²), so the weight of wool allowing 225 g per 31 cm² (8 oz per 1 ft²) was about 1·25 kg (2¾ lb).

Whatever way you buy the wool, it is always prudent to get rather more than is absolutely necessary since you cannot exactly judge the quantities of each colour.

A suggested colour scheme is shown in figure 31:

Edging and dividers: chocolate brown
Small slanting pattern: orange, green and golden yellow shades
All outlining: tan and dark orange
Border background: darkish greens
Border diamonds: lightish orange and golds, contrasting centre crosses
Field background: light greens
Stripes in centre diamond: different greens for each, light and dark alternately
Centre motif: dark green, orange or gold cross
Diamonds in field: orange and gold shades, contrasting crosses

Some of the field colours should appear in the borders, otherwise the two will look disconnected. In this design they worked in quite easily. Before ordering wool it is a good plan to draw the design out roughly on a small scale (one-third or one-quarter size) and to colour it in to see how it looks. Adjustments are more easily made at this stage than later.

The wool can be bought as broken hanks, but much more cheaply as thrums, and 2 kg (4½ lb) of a tan/orange/green mixture should be asked for. This quantity will ensure that there is enough of the main colours, and any extra shades could easily be worked into the small diamonds or into the stripes of the large central motif. This mixture might have very little or no chocolate brown, so that could be ordered separately or the darkest tan or green could be used instead for the edging and dividers.

All the colours in a batch of thrums work in together in good proportions, so unless the exact colour is important, alternatives could include blues/fawns/pinks or dark browns/ orange/yellows. On arrival, sort the wool out into different colours and see how it may best be used in the design.

There should be wool left over from this amount to go into stock, and this can be used for trying out colour combinations the next time you plan a rug.

An alternative design within the same border is also charted (figure 32). This has a more complicated pattern, but the same range of colours could be used to make an equally pleasant rug. These designs illustrate how the initial idea can be developed in different ways. A pencil, some scrap paper and some doodling will produce many more.

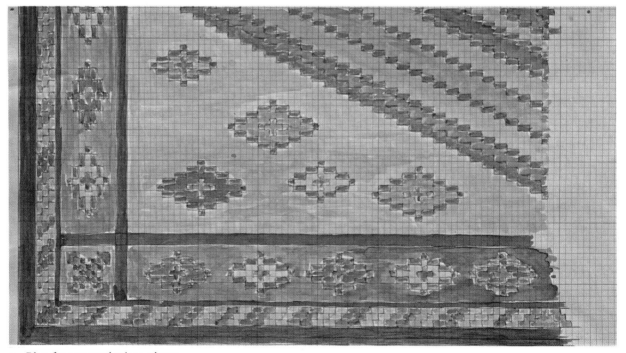

31 Plan for suggested colour scheme

A pile rug in a modern design made up from a batch of mixed thrums.

It may be interesting to note that the original scheme for the border on this rug had been a two-stitch slanting pattern and true diamonds, taking up 13 stitches which together with the dividers would have made 20 stitches in all, leaving 67 across the field for the centre pattern. In the alternative design, the diamonds planned for the centre were just the right height, as three fitted into the length of the field, but were so wide that they fitted too exactly into the remaining width, giving a cramped effect. The design needed amending and there were several choices:

1 Omit the slanting pattern and one stitch divider and move the true diamonds out to the edge, so gaining an extra three stitches at each side of the field.

2 Reduce the size of the centre diamonds and leave the border as planned.

3 Alter the border diamonds to make them thinner and make the slanting pattern one stitch wider.

Any of these would have been quite possible but the third possibility was chosen as the best. This illustrates how a design, once planned in outline, can be varied in detail so that the idea can be improved on.

When making pile rugs from a chart, it is easy to lose track of which line of knots is being worked. A long ruler laid on the chart just above this line, so that the highest row visible is the one in use, helps a great deal.

If you are making a rug with a symmetrical pattern and there is a chance that one of the colours may run short, it is wise to divide each shade into two halves by weight and then to put away one half to use for the second half of the work. If a shortage looms up as the work progresses the colour scheme may be altered in good time, but if this is only realized when the rug is more than half finished it is too late to balance the colours.

In the Turkey knot rug, the mid-green used at each end had been planned for the whole of the background outside the large diamond in the centre, but the half-ration was used up long before reaching the half-way mark on the pattern. The colouring was amended quite successfully but nothing could have been done to save the situation if more than half the rug had been worked and there had been no

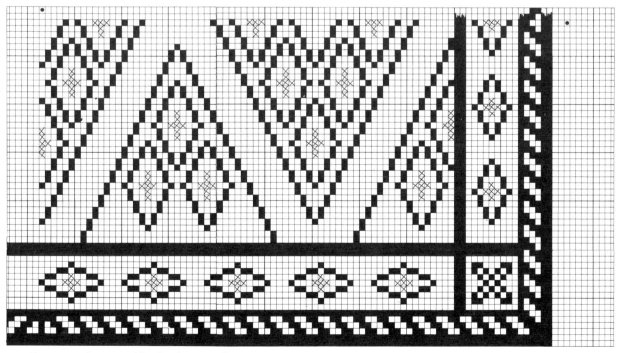

32 Alternative design used border shown in figure 31

125

matching wool available to finish.

The crescent rug used a combination of pile and flat stitches which produces a three dimensional effect. The wavy edging, main crescents, dots and centre area were worked in Surrey stitch, the inner crescents in rice stitch and the background in long-legged cross stitch. It is difficult to work the flat stitches close up to Surrey stitch since the pile gets in the way, so the background was done first and the Surrey stitch afterwards. It is easy to work a motif and then fill in the background. On the other hand, great concentration is needed to leave a space for the motif while the background is being worked.

The whole of the rug design is in tones of turquoise blue and the shape of the space down the centre between the crescents has been accentuated by using a coral colour. The crescent motifs were not outlined and their relative importance in the design was consequently reduced. This effect would be reversed if the crescents were to be outlined and the centre spaces simply treated as part of the background to the pattern.

The small Surrey stitch pile rug was a development of the jotting from an old one. It has almost turned into a sampler as three border patterns were tried out. The slant of the small pattern would be better changed in the centre of the line for matching corners. The economy of

colours (dark turquoise to light, and and browns shading to gold) has a pleasing result.

All these tiny rugs are examples of different stitches and they were made that size for ease of carrying. The designs would be equally satisfactory if repeated over a wider area.

The Kuba Dagestan rug, whose octagons and ribbon edging were used in the little Soumak, also yielded the design for the unfinished rug. The original was worked at about 10 knots per 2·5 cm (1 in), and although it would be quite possible to use 10s canvas and Brussels thrums to make a rug on the same scale, the time involved ruled out this idea. It was decided to work the rug on 8s canvas in Surrey stitch, using 2-ply Axminster wool, and as the width was to be 69 cm (27 in) some of the canvas was cut off and a new selvedge made.

From the original rug four motifs were selected for the field and arranged in alternate rows, while only one of the border patterns could be fitted into the available width. This motif was not turned to go across the ends as a little extra length was welcome, so the end borders are rather wider than those down the sides.

The chevron edging on the border, the dividers and most of the outlining was worked in charcoal. Since there may not be enough wool for the edging plait and the

An unfinished rug worked in an intricate pattern. Lengths of different coloured thread show the various shades in use.

flat-stitch ends as well, these are worked after the rest of the rug is finished, and might have to be in another dark shade. About 5 cm (2 in) of canvas was left free of pile at each end so that there would be space to work initials and a date, which were impossible to fit anywhere in the design itself. They will be done in cross stitch and the rest of the area filled by long-legged cross stitch.

Canvas widths

Occasionally it happens that there is no canvas in exactly the width required; this is particularly so with 8s which at present is only available in 91 cm (36 in) width. If needed in a narrower width, count the number of bars required across the canvas and allow two or three more to balance the width of the uncut selvedge. Run a thread in to mark the place and double check the count. Cut off and machine up and down the length twice. Then machine a narrow binding over the cut edge, so making an artificial selvedge on that side. The discarded strip will be useful for trying out designs and colours.

A chart worked out for a flat stitch or a pile rug can also be used for Soumak stitch if it is remembered

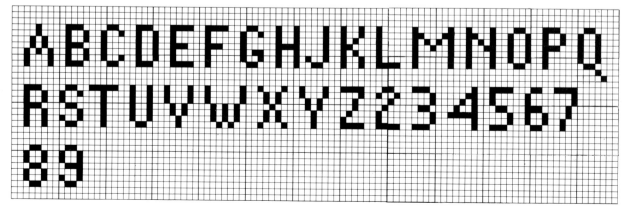

33 Initials and numbers planned on graph paper

that a bar of canvas must be gained on one selvedge to allow for the extra width needed by the top stitch in each line. If the canvas is being cut as described, allow an extra bar when counting.

For a rug wider than any of the available canvases, two widths must be joined by stitching the selvedges. These are both bent back to the underside, and the inner selvedge thread on each is sewn tightly together. This makes an extra double bar of canvas with the two selvedges sticking out behind. The stitching must be done very firmly. Take care with the accurate lining-up of the canvas to ensure that the join is invisible and that the pattern matches.

To allow for the working of this new bar, the chart needs an extra square in the width. With 109 bars in each strip of canvas, the charts must have 219 squares in all; one of

109 and one of 110. The method is to complete the rug to within three bars of the selvedge on each strip and then join them as indicated. There will then be seven bars to finish. After these have been worked over, the selvedges at the back are pressed out and if necessary stitched down. Both width and lengthwise joins may also be made by the overlap method.

Finishing the rug

It might seem that to line a finished rug would be to complete the job perfectly, but this is not so. If a rug is lined all the grit and dirt which inevitably works through to the underside will be trapped there and gradually wear away the backs of the knots or stitches. It is much better to be able to sweep it all up when the rug is lifted.

All initials except Q can be worked over seven stitches, so their height is just under 2·5 cm (1 in) using 8s canvas (figure 33). Unless you are making a special feature of them, choose a colour that is visible against the background but does not draw attention to itself. If they are to be important in the design, the size may be increased and the colour made more positive.

One of the things which makes old samplers so interesting is that they are almost always signed and dated, and in this way have a history and an identity for future generations. Since a rug treated with ordinary care is quite likely to last for 150 years or more, it is worth giving serious consideration to the inclusion in the design of initials, or even a whole name, and a date.

Most of the things you buy or make nowadays have a fairly short useful life and are then discarded. In making a rug you are truly making your own heirloom.

Suppliers of wools, canvases and needles

2-ply carpet wool	Jackson's Rugcraft Ltd, Croft Mill, Hebden Bridge, Yorkshire
	Royal Wilton Carpet Factory, (The Weaver's Shop), Wilton, Salisbury, Wiltshire
	Winwood Textiles Ltd, P O Box 27, Lisle Avenue, Kidderminster
(thrums only)	Hugh Mackay & Co Ltd, P O Box No 1, Durham City
Brussels thrums	Spinning Jenny, Bradley via Keighley, Yorkshire
4s and 5s canvas	Jackson's Rugcraft Ltd, Croft Mill, Hebden Bridge, Yorkshire
	Royal Wilton Carpet Factory, (The Weaver's Shop), Wilton, Salisbury, Wiltshire
	Harrods Limited, Knightsbridge, London SW1
	Spinning Jenny, Bradley via Keighley, Yorkshire
needles	Royal Wilton Carpet Factory, (The Weaver's Shop), Wilton, Salisbury, Wiltshire
	Jackson's Rugcraft Ltd, Croft Mill, Hebden Bridge, Yorkshire
	Spinning Jenny, Bradley via Keighley, Yorkshire

Conversion Table

All weights and measures in this book are given in the metric system, followed by the imperial in brackets. Conversions are correctly adjusted within one system and have been taken up or down to round figures in all instances to make for ease of working. Do not worry if you find the conversions differ slightly from those given in the table below, which is for general reference. Provided you follow one set of measures—*either* the imperial *or* the metric—these variations are of no importance.

Linear measures

Metric	Imperial
6 mm	$\frac{1}{4}$ in
13 mm	$\frac{1}{2}$ in
19 mm	$\frac{3}{4}$ in
2·5 cm	1 in
5 cm	2 in
7·5 cm	3 in
10 cm	4 in
12·5 cm	5 in
15 cm	6 in
30·5 cm	1 foot
91·5 cm	1 yard
1 metre	1·093 yards

Glossary

all over design   a design that is repeated throughout a piece of work.

appliqué or applied work   pieces of fabric or thick threads applied to a background fabric and held down by stitching.

automatic patterns   embroidery patterns either built into a machine or worked by auxiliary pattern cams.

Axminster wool   type of 2-ply wool used in carpet making.

backing   material or paper, placed behind work to reinforce certain stitches, and which can later be removed.

balance wheel   wheel at right hand end of machine enabling needle to be moved by hand rotation.

bars   alternative term for warp and weft threads of canvas.

to baste   to tack.

Berlin star   design used in canvas work.

bias strip   strip of fabric cut across the grain.

to bind   to cover edges of work by holding two or more layers together to form a decorative edge.

bobbin   circular spool for holding bottom thread on modern sewing machine.

Brussels thrum   thrum of fine double-strand wool.

buckram   a coarse linen or cloth stiffened with gum or paste.

calico   plain unprinted cotton cloth originally imported from the East.

canvas   cloth woven in regular open meshes, the grade of which is determined by the number of threads to the inch.

chain stitcher   a substitute for the bobbin case in some sewing machines to make the chain stitch.

chevron edging   zigzag edging in two colours.

chintz   a type of glazed cotton cloth printed in colour-fast patterns and designs.

circular stitcher   a device screwed to the sewing machine bed as an aid to stitching in circles.

Coscote method   a method of joining patches with a sewing machine using a swing needle.

cover plate   a smooth metal plate which covers the feed teeth of a sewing machine, allowing free movement of the fabric under the sewing foot.

crewel wool   a thin worsted yarn used for embroidery and tapestry work.

to darn (machine)	to machine freely with the presser foot removed and the feed teeth covered by the cover plate, while the fabric is stretched in an embroidery frame.
darning foot	sewing machine attachment which allows free sewing without the control of the feed teeth.
divider	a line of stitches between different border patterns in stitched rug-making.
Domette	a type of wool interlining.
dressmaker's pencil	a pencil specially constituted for the safe marking of fabrics.
dressmaker's tracing paper	paper specially treated for transferring markings on to fabrics.
Dupion	a trade name for light fabric with a roughened silk-like texture.
edging plait	method of finishing and securing rough edges of canvas in stitched rug-making.
embroidery frame	a double circular frame of wood, metal or plastic, sometimes with adjustable screw, for holding material taut for free embroidery.
eyelet stitcher	a device added to, or exchanged with, the needleplate of a sewing machine for sewing eyelets.
feed or feed dog	a row of teeth beneath the needle of a sewing machine, which controls the stitch length and the movement of the cloth.
flat bed machine	a sewing machine without a free arm.
flower stitcher	a fitting used instead of the presser foot on some sewing machines to sew small circles or flower patterns.
foundation	a fine cotton or muslin backing to which strips of patchwork are sewn.
to frame up	to prepare a canvas in a stretching frame.
free arm machine	a sewing machine with a space beneath the base which allows for fabrics to be passed round it. This facility is useful for stitching tubular items such as sleeves. Such a machine may also have a moveable extension for additional ease of working.
free embroidery	this is worked in an embroidery frame with a sewing machine set for darning.
georgette	a type of thin silk dress fabric.
gingham	a type of cotton or linen cloth, often woven in stripes or checks.
goldsmith	a type of gold thread used for embroidery.
gusset	a piece of material let into an article to strengthen or enlarge it.
hank	a coil or skein of wool for use in rug-making.
hemstitching needle	a sewing machine needle with one or two metal wings for making holes when fabric is pierced. A twin needle version is also available.
hessian	a strong, coarse woven cloth of the type often used for sacking.
holes	the space between warp and weft bars, or threads, of a canvas.
hoop	an alternative term for an embroidery frame.
isometric paper	printed paper bearing a geometric complex of lines of equal length on which designs for hexagons, diamonds and triangles can be accurately drawn.
Italian quilting	a type of decorative quilting, worked by hand or machine, using two layers of fabric.
knotting or tying	anchoring two or more layers of material to avoid ballooning.
lawn	a kind of fine linen resembling cambric.
lining	fabric, usually cotton, used as backing for a piece of work.
log cabin	a traditional North American patchwork design made up of long thin patches, laid one upon the other to resemble the construction of a log cabin.
meander	a winding pattern, used in rug-making, usually incorporating flowers and leaves.
mixed thrum	a batch of factory left-overs of wool in a variety of colours.
motif	a feature of a design or pattern which is either the central point of attention or used repeatedly throughout the design.
organdie	a fine, translucent kind of muslin.
padding	a middle layer or interlining of sheepswool, cotton or synthetic wadding, placed between the top side and backing of a quilt.
pieced patchwork	a patchwork made up of pieces of fabric sewn together to form a mathematical pattern.
pineapple pattern	a traditional patchwork design based on the log cabin.
piping	a type of cord used to finish off and give a tailored edge to a piece of work. The piping is usually covered with matching or contrasting fabric

piqué	a stiff cotton fabric bearing a raised pattern, formed in weaving.
poplin	a mixed woven fabric of mercerized cotton.
presser bar	a fitting which controls the pressure on the presser foot of a sewing machine. The presser bar lever lowers the foot and engages the top tension.
presser foot	standard foot for normal sewing on a machine.
quilting	the process of joining two or more layers of material together with a decorative stitch.
quilting frame	an adjustable wooden frame over which quilting is held taut during working.
reverse appliqué	a design machine stitched through two or more layers of material, parts of which are cut away to reveal the different levels beneath.
rug or carpet fork	a utensil with which to sew down looped threads to form a tufted or pile surface.
Rya	a Scandinavian type of rug with a shaggy pile.
to scrabble	to tease the surface of a pile rug in the direction in which it lies, to remove loose fluff.
scrim	a type of thin canvas used for lining.
selvedge	the woven edge of a piece of material bonded to avoid fraying.
shuttle	an elongated spool for holding the bottom thread on an old sewing machine.
silversmith	a type of silver thread used in embroidery.
slubbed	wool slightly twisted (for spinning).
solid template	a template made of metal or firm card used for marking the exact size and shape of a piece of fabric to be used as a patch.
spiral stitcher	a device substituted on some sewing machines for the presser foot for sewing decorative spiral patterns.
square or slate frame	a frame made from two stout pieces of wood with webbing attached and pegs for stretching a canvas.
straight stitch machine	a sewing machine that will only sew in a straight line, forwards and backwards.
stranded cotton	cotton embroidery thread sold in lengths already cut.
stranded embroidery silk	silk embroidery thread sold in lengths already cut.

strawboard	a coarse yellow millboard made from straw pulp.
swing needle machine	a sewing machine that will sew from side to side as well as in straight lines, producing zigzag and satin stitches.
tailor's chalk	a type of chalk made specifically for marking fabric.
tailor tacking foot	an attachment available on some sewing machines which allows both spaced and close loops to be made as an aid to dressmaking and as a decorative stitch for embroidery.
tambour	a type of frame used for holding fabric while embroidering.
template	a firm guide around which material is marked or cut.
thread	alternative term for bar when defining the warp and weft strands of a canvas; silk, cotton or synthetic fibre used for hand and machine stitching and embroidery.
thrum	a batch of wool made up from factory left overs.
triple needle	a shank bearing three identical needles for sewing a triple line of stitching at the same time on some sewing machines.
twin needle	a shank bearing two identical needles for stitching a twin line of stitches at the same time on some sewing machines.
under braider	a plate with a ridged groove through which cord or braid can be fed when screwed down on to the sewing machine bed.
vanishing muslin	a fabric used as a backing which can either be torn off or ironed away afterwards.
Vee pattern	a traditional patchwork design based on the log cabin.
Velcro strip	a trade name for a fastening strip made in two sections: one portion has a velvet finish, the other a hooked surface which adheres when the two sections are pressed together.
warp bar or thread	that lying parallel to the selvedges of a canvas or fabric.
weft bar or thread	that lying at right angles to the selvedges of a canvas or fabric.
width knob or lever	controls stitch width on a swing needle sewing machine.
window	a transparent template for determining the size of a patch including the allowance for turning.
wing needle	a term for hemstitching needle.

Index

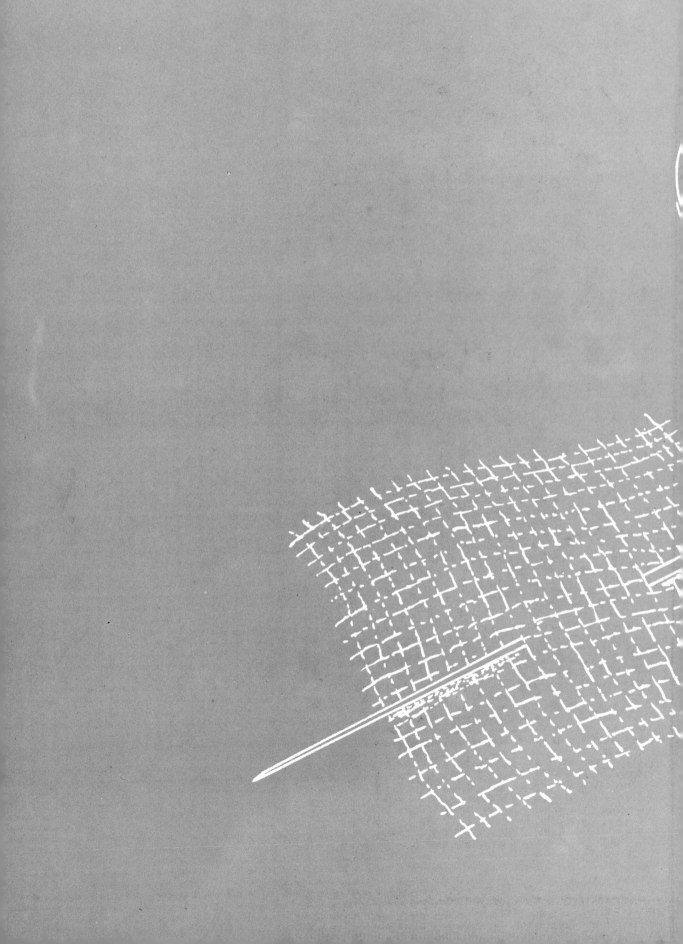